Routledge Revivals

Strategic Materials

When this book was originally published in 1984 there was little published data on the extraction or exploitation of strategic materials. The book surveys the entire range of strategic materials and considers both the economics of their extraction and the political issues involved in safeguarding Western access to these critical materials – issues which remain very pertinent in the 21st century and in an era of geopolitical turbulence.

The book begins with a discussion of the mining processes and examines the implications of the by-product nature of many strategic materials for the mining enterprise. The possibilities of stretching existing supplies by either substituting other materials or recycling are also investigated. Finally, in an assessment of the marketing and pricing of strategic materials, there is discussion of the possibility of OPEC-type cartels developing and the political risks associated with this are considered. *Strategic Materials: A World Survey* brings together various strands of the debate surrounding strategic materials and has established itself as an important work in the field.

Strategic Materials

A World Survey

Rae Weston

Routledge
Taylor & Francis Group

First published in Great Britain in 1984 by Croom Helm Ltd

This edition first published in 2026 by Routledge
4 Park Square, Milton Park, Abingdon, Oxon, OX14 4RN

and by Routledge
605 Third Avenue, New York, NY 10158

Routledge is an imprint of the Taylor & Francis Group, an informa business

For Product Safety Concerns and Information please contact our EU representative GPSR@taylorandfrancis.com. Taylor & Francis Verlag GmbH, Kaufingerstraße 24, 80331 München, Germany

ISBN: 978-1-041-35345-4 (hbk)
ISBN: 978-1-003-79729-6 (ebk)
ISBN: 978-1-041-35347-8 (pbk)

Book DOI 10.4324/9781003797296

STRATEGIC MATERIALS

A WORLD SURVEY

Rae Weston

CROOM HELM
London & Sydney

Croom Helm Ltd, Provident House, Burrell Row,
Beckenham, Kent BR3 1AT
Croom Helm Australia Pty Ltd, First Floor,
139 King Street, Sydney, NSW 2001, Australia

British Library Cataloguing in Publication Data

Weston, Rae
Strategic materials.
1. Natural resources 2. World politics – 1975-1985
I. Title
333.7 HC55

ISBN 0-7099-2740-1

ROWMAN & ALLANHELD

Published in the United States of America in 1984
by Rowman & Allanheld, Publishers
(A division of Littlefield, Adams & Company)
81 Adams Drive, Totowa, New Jersey 07512

Library of Congress Cataloging in Publication Data

Weston, Rae.
Strategic materials.

Bibliography: p.
Includes index.
1. Mineral industries. 2. Strategic materials.
3. Mineral industries–Government policy–United States.
4. Strategic materials–Government policy–United States.
5. Mines and mineral resources. I. Title.
HD9506.A2W47 1984 333.8'5 84-3358
ISBN 0-86598-165-5 (Rowman & Allanheld)

Printed and bound in Great Britain

CONTENTS

PREFACE

The purpose of this book is to highlight some aspects of the strategic materials debate that appear to have been overlooked. Major focus in that debate has been on the possibility of a supply disruption due to political events in a major producing country. It is suggested in this contribution that the existence of stockpiles threatens prices of these materials and inhibits supply and ought to be replaced for many of these materials with sponsorship of the development of potential new sources. This would be a better strategy for ensuring continued availability of these materials. A second threat to stable supplies arises from the pricing and marketing arrangements for these materials which allow the possibility of manipulation to be a potential problem.

Chapter 1 discusses why some materials are regarded as 'strategic' and the significance of that description. In Chapter 2 each of the strategic materials identified in the first chapter is described and the range of existing and potential uses of each is examined. The dependence of demand for a number of strategic materials on only a few industries is clear from this examination. Chapter 3 focuses on the existing and potential sources of supply for the strategic materials, while Chapter 4 investigates the possibilities of stretching the supplies of these materials by recycling or by the substitution of other materials. Chapter 5 examines the possibilities of supply disruptions or restrictions, the problem of stockpiles and the likelihood of cartels. The difficult and often-neglected area of pricing and markets is the focus of Chapter 6. The combination of small, thin markets, government stockpiles and the possible private sector holdings of these materials threatens to make many of these markets unstable and more readily able to be manipulated.

Risk aspects of the individual strategic materials are summarised in the conclusion and the prospects for future crisis situations in particular materials is discussed.

Most of this book was written while I was a visiting professor in the Department of Economics at the University of Western Ontario in 1981. The research on which the book is based relied on the resources of the Hargrave Library at Monash University, the Colorado School of Mines and the South African Bureau of Mines. Many companies and government agencies have been very helpful in my acquisition of information. Debate between mining company representatives and trade representatives at the April 1981 Metal Bulletin Conference, South African Minerals and Metals in a World Context, in Johannesburg led me to thinking about the marketing and pricing aspects of strategic materials. A visit to Rustenburg Platinum Mines during the same conference which included inspection of the Merensky Reef at the mine face has been of assistance to the development of this book and to *Platinum: A World Survey* (forthcoming). My thanks to all of the above.

Rae Weston

1 STRATEGIC MATERIALS – WHY ARE THEY STRATEGIC?

In the aftermath of the oil crisis of the 1970s, it is surprising to find that an even greater area of vulnerability is not widely known or appreciated, although this vulnerability is greater and present for more countries than any produced or highlighted by OPEC. This vulnerability lies in the area described as 'strategic materials'.

Part of the lack of awareness here may be accounted for by the failure of governments concerned with building stockpiles of these materials, and of commentators discussing the need for and adequacy of government plans, to define the term 'strategic materials' in any consistent way.

Originally the word 'strategic' meant 'essential to effective military strategy' but it appears to be used now in a wider sense. The Head of Minerals Strategy at the Institute of Geological Sciences in London, A.A. Archer, speaking at a symposium on 'The Availability of Strategic Materials' in November 1979 argued that the word 'strategic' was used so ambiguously that it ought to be abandoned in favour of more precise terms like 'criticality' and 'vulnerability'.

In fact both 'strategic' and 'critical' are used in Section 12 (1) of the United States *Strategic and Critical Materials Stock Piling Act* (50 U.S.C. 98 *et seq.*) which provides

> The term 'strategic and critical materials' means materials that
> (A) would be needed to supply the military, industrial and essential civilian needs of the United States during a national emergency, and
> (B) are not found or produced in the United States in sufficient quantities to meet such need.

To take four specific examples, the world's reserves of platinum group metals, vanadium, manganese ore and chrome ore are located overwhelmingly in only two countries – South Africa and the USSR. All four materials are regarded as important in industrial and/or military production and all have some uses for which no feasible alternative exists.

It must be emphasised, however, that there is no real consensus on the ambit of strategic materials. Table A1.1 summarises the materials of the US strategic stockpile – a total of 60 materials or groups of materials; Gordon McLendon (1980) lists 31 strategic materials; the Sinclair Securities Company (1980) lists 18 strategic materials; and International Strategic Metals Ltd (1981) lists 24 'major' strategic materials (all US stockpile only). For countries outside the United States, the contents of their strategic stockpiles may vary considerably from those included in any of the above lists.

For the purposes of the present study, the following materials will be included in the definition of 'strategic materials':

antimony	indium	selenium
beryllium	lithium	tantalum
cadmium	manganese	tellurium
chromium	mercury	titanium
cobalt	molybdenum	tungsten
columbium (niobium)	nickel	vanadium
germanium	platinum group metals	zirconium
hafnium	rhenium	

In 1980 the American Geological Institute warned that the USSR was trying to halt or interrupt US access to minerals critical to national defence, at a time when US stockpiles of over 90 strategic materials were as much as 80 per cent short of their goals. The central point of the Institute's expression of concern was that the position of the stockpile left the United States vulnerable. Vulnerability refers here not only to the comparatively stronger position of the Soviet bloc with respect to these materials but also to the dependence of the USA, for supplies of certain materials, on only a few countries, including some whose continued political stability may be subject to doubt.

This second aspect of vulnerability is shared by other industrialised countries. Table 1.1 shows the importance of South Africa as a source of supply of various strategic materials for the USA, UK, Japan and West Germany; Table 1.2 indicates the net import reliance of the United States for selected strategic materials for the 1975-8 period.

Representative Jim Santini described the US dependence on southern Africa as follows:

> The U.S. is dependent on southern Africa for approximately three-fourths of its supply of manganese, cobalt and chrome. If the Soviet Union knocks off Zaire, if Zimbabwe goes down the drain – Zambia is already a Marxist State – and if South Africa has a racial revo-

Table 1.1: South Africa's Role in World Mineral Reserves and Production and the Import Dependency of Western Industrial Countries on South African Supplies: 1979

Mineral Commodity	Reserves South Africa (metric tons)	Of Western World Reserves		Of World Reserves		Production South Africa (metric tons)	Of Western World Production		Of World Production		Import Dependency of Industrialised countries			
		Rank	%	Rank	%		Rank	%	Rank	%	Japan	USA	UK	West Germany
Antimony (metal)	3000,000	2	18	3	5	11,850	2	24	3	16	—	6	90	15
Chrome ore	3.096 million (300m depth)	1	84	1	81	3,689,178	1	56	1	36	52	48	79	66
Cobalt	70,000	5	5	7	4									
Nickel	5.83 million (600m depth)	5	8	7	6		5	5	7	4	18	4	—	17
Manganese ore	12,139.8 million	1	93	1	78	5,237,255	1	42	2	22	4 ore; 31 metal and ferron	35 ore and metal	46 ore; 74 metal	23 ore; 52 metal
Platinum group metals	30,200 (600m depth)	1	89	1	75	Ø	1	92	1	51	28	55	58	9
Titanium (metal)	33,256,000	3	17	3	15	Ø	3	17	3	15				
Vanadium	7,760,000 (30m depth)	1	90	1	49	Ø	1	61	1	45	90	87	—	16
Zirconium	4,000,000	2	12	4	10	Ø	3	9	na	na	7	1	7	16

Notes: Ø = classified data; na = not available.
Source: Mineral Bureau (1980).

Table 1.2: Net Import Reliance of the United States for Selected Strategic Materials, 1975-8

Material	Net Import Reliance as % of Apparent Consumption
Antimony	43
Cadmium	66
Chromium	90
Cobalt	90
Columbium	100
Manganese	98
Mercury	62
Nickel	77
Platinum group metals	89
Selenium	40
Tantalum	96
Titanium	46
Tungsten	59

Source: US Bureau of Mines (1981).

lution or invasion or both, Russia will control 80% of the market place of these three strategic minerals.

Table 1.3 shows the reserves of South Africa (and the USSR) as percentages of the world's known reserves of a number of minerals, figures which make it clear that the matter is not only of concern to the the United States.

France analysed its own vulnerability with respect to mineral materials in the early 1970s and classified its position as shown in Table 1.4. In January 1975 France budgeted 250 million francs for the establishment of precautionary stockpiles equal to two months' stocks, managed by GIRM, the centralised purchasing agency. (A Committee, including industry representatives, advises the Ministry of Industry on whose behalf GIRM acts.)

West Germany's concern has been with its vulnerability in five minerals – chromium, vanadium, cobalt, manganese and blue asbestos – and with industry's stocks estimated at four months' supplies, the government's objective has been to have these private stocks revised to approximately one year's supply with the government able to use these in a crisis, in exchange for subsidies towards financing charges and guarantees against book losses. The scheme involves the Deutsche Bundesbank providing DM60 million a year to be used for refinancing which will subsidise stockpile financing costs by two-thirds.

Table 1.3: Reserves of South Africa and the USSR as Percentages of the World's Reserves of Various Minerals

Mineral	South Africa's % of World Reserves	USSR's % of World Reserves	Combined South African and USSR %age
Platinum group metals	86	13	99
Vanadium	64	33	97
Manganese ore	48	45	93
Chrome ore	83	1	84
Gold	49	19	68
Titanium	5	16	21
Nickel	10	7	17

Source: Van Rensburg and Pretorius (1977), p. 136.

Table 1.4: France: Vulnerability in Mineral Materials

Degree of Vulnerability	Mineral Material
Very great	silver, platinum, diamonds, phosphate zirconium, titanium, cobalt, vanadium
Great	antimony, copper, manganese, molybdenum, tungsten
Medium	bauxite, chrome, tin
Weak	iron, nickel, lead, zinc, potash

Source: *Mining Magazine* (June 1980), p. 547.

In the United Kingdom the government has been under pressure to establish emergency stockpiles of metals essential to keep the steel industry operating in times of unexpected shortage; and in Japan, Satsuo Takashima, president of the Japanese Mining Association, has expressed hopes that strategic stockpiling of the US type would be adopted.

Canada, though itself a main supplier of many metals and minerals, is vulnerable to supply disruptions and a recent study by the Mineral Supply Branch of Energy, Mines and Resources recommended that emergency plans should be developed to cope with brief supply disruptions; that strategies be developed to reduce Canadian dependence on imported materials in the medium to long term; and to develop Canada's self-reliance in minerals in the long term.

Quite apart from the dependence on a few sources for supplies of a number of strategic materials, many of these materials are only produced as by-products of other mining or processing. This dependence of the production of many strategic materials on the primary production of another metal has a serious impact on the ability of the supply of these by-product materials to respond to change in demand that are reflected in changes in price. It is not suggested that even base minerals are highly price responsive at close-to-capacity production levels, but primary metals will respond with an increase in supply over time as rising prices make viable known, but not previously mined, deposits and encourage exploration to identify new deposits. For by-product materials a rise in prices alone will not be sufficient to generate increases in supply and there may well be shortages that persist for some time.

Table 1.5 lists the main supply associations of the strategic materials. Most are derived as by-products of the four base metals: copper,

Table 1.5: Product Association of the Strategic Materials

Antimony

Primarily derived from stibnite ore usually associated with gold, antimony is also produced as a lead-smelting by-product.

Beryllium

Apart from the US operations where beryllium is produced from deposits of bertrandite, all other sources are from beryl ore which is not sufficiently concentrated to be mined by itself and it is produced as a by-product of molybdenum or lithium or of gem-type beryl.

Cadmium

No commercial ore-bodies of cadmium are known; it is recovered entirely as a by-product of zinc smelting and refining.

Chromium

Chromium is obtained from chromite or chrome iron ore.

Cobalt

Only mined specifically in some Moroccan mines; in other mines it is a by-product of nickel, copper and zinc ores.

Columbium

Columbite is not found in a naturally occurring pure form and it is usually won as a by-product or co-product from tin mining and often with tantalum.

Indium

Indium is a minor by-product of lead and zinc smelting and refining.

Germanium

Germanium is produced as a minor by-product of zinc ores.

Hafnium

Hafnium is recovered as a by-product in the production of hafnium-free nuclear-grade zirconium base alloys.

Lithium

Lithium is proudced as the major product from pegmatite ores and from brine.

Manganese

Manganese ores are mined as the sole product from their sources.

Mercury

While mercury is primarily won as the minor part of cinnabar, the deposits of cinnabar are mined for their mercury content alone.

Molybdenum

Porphyry molybdenum deposits are major sources, but molybdenum is also derived from copper-molybdenum deposits or as a copper by-product.

Nickel

Nickel is mainly derived from nickel-copper or iron sulphides and the deposits often contain other metals such as cobalt, silver, gold, platinum group metals, selenium and tellurium.

Platinum Group Metals

South Africa is the only country that mines platinum as a primary mineral. In the USSR platinum is produced as a by-product of palladium (with twice as much palladium as platinum produced). Canada's platinum is produced as a by-product of its nickel mining.

Rhenium

Commercial rhenium production is derived from molybdenite from porphyry deposits of copper or copper-molybdenum.

Selenium

The main producers of selenium recover it from the copper refining process as a by-product.

Tantalum

Only a few producers mine specifically to obtain tantalum-containing minerals, the majority produce tantalite as a by-product of tin mining or from tin slags or from a columbite-tantalite combination.

Tellurium

The metal is mainly derived as a by-product of copper and lead refining and its supply is mostly limited to that available from copper output.

Titanium

Titanium is derived from beach sand deposits containing ilmenite and rutile. In some less important sources ilmenite or zircon is recovered as a co-product of tin-dredging or in association with thorium and iron as rare earth.

Tungsten

Tungsten is produced from its own ores — wolfram and scheelite — as the primary product.

Vanadium

In the USSR vanadium is produced from vanadium-rich slag, a co-product with iron. Other main sources are titanium-bearing magnetites or as a uranium, iron or phosphorus by-product.

Zirconium

Zirconium is produced from the mineral zircon which is mined from beach sands that contain ilmenite, rutile and other minerals as well as zircon.

---

lead, zinc and tin. There are some strategic materials that are mined on their own, of which mercury and tungsten are perhaps the most important, but some others like germanium and rhenium occur as such minimal fractions of another metal ore that their recovery requires the accumulation of huge quantities of residual material at refineries or smelters. Hafnium is one of the materials that is derived as a by-product of a mineral recovered from the production of another mineral.

Table 1.6 indicates the relative importance of by-product metals to major copper producers in 1973 and 1979; and Table 1.7 examines the specific case of Bougainville Copper where the by-product, gold, had reached virtually joint-product status in 1980.

Table 1.6: Relative Importance of By-product Metals to Major Copper Producers

	% of Total Production Costs	
	1973	1979
Australia	47	82
Canada	78	82
Chile	6	22
Papua New Guinea	48	76
Peru	10	28
Philippines	23	32
South Africa	31	49
USA	29	41
Zaire	26	66
Zambia	7	19

Source: Stewart (1981).

Table 1.7: Relative Contributions to Value of Production: Bougainville Copper (%)

	Copper	Gold	Silver
1972	83	16	1
1973	83	16	1
1974	74	25	1
1975	69	29	2
1976	74	24	2
1977	66	32	2
1978	64	34	2
1979	60	37	3
1980	51	46	3

Source: Bougainville Copper Ltd, *Annual Report* (1980).

While it is clear from Tables 1.6 and 1.7 that by-products are able to provide producers with a hedge against downturns in the market for their main product, that advantage is not consistently or reliably obtained. In 1980, 42 per cent of the value of base metals was recovered by by-products. Even for the decade of the 1970s some by-products, including cadmium, selenium and vanadium, provided a lower return than the base metals with which they were associated, and others like nickel, cobalt and molybdenum had strong price surges but equally strong price falls.

There are several reactions possible to the increased value of a by-product material. First, recovery of the by-product could be improved or increased. Shirley (1979) examines ways in which copper producers might improve their molybdenite recovery and suggests that primary molybdenite recovery could be improved if producers add an oil type collector to their primary grinding circuit in milling. This addition has adverse effects on either the grade of copper concentrates or on the recovery of copper or both, but at high molybdenum and low copper prices that might be an economic tradeoff.

A second possibility is that new by-product sources that were previously uneconomic may now become sources of production. For example, germanium is mainly derived as a minor by-product of certain zinc ores, but there is potentially a large supply of germanium recoverable from the ash and flue dusts resulting from the combustion of coal in power generation. At high prices and with fairly small supplies available from the usual sources, this potential supply may well be converted into actual production.

A third possibility is that producers who regard by-product outputs as free bonuses and deduct the revenue from them from the total production costs of the mine, may use this inaccurate reflection of the actual costs of production as the basis for expanding capacity. Parkinson (1980) argues that this situation may lead to the main products' output increasing at a greater rate than either its cost or the market situation justifies and developing into a 'loss-leader'. He attributes this result to the costing practices within the mining industry which lead to production cost figures for the main product being quoted after credit is allowed for by-product revenue. This results in inaccurate production cost figures for both the main product and the by-product.

2 THE ANATOMY OF STRATEGIC MATERIALS

In this chapter the strategic materials are described individually and the range of existing and potential uses of each of them is discussed. It will be seen from this discussion that the demand for a number of strategic materials is derived from only a few industries. The extreme example is rhenium, the demand for which is almost entirely for catalysts in low-lead or lead-free gasolines. The more widespread the use of a material, as in the case of molybdenum, the less vulnerable it is to replacement by some technological advance.

Antimony (Sb)

The word antimony is derived from the Greek *anti monos*, a metal seldom found alone, a description appropriate not only to its mineralogical association with other ores but also in its modern day usage which has been in association with other elements.

Known at least since Biblical times, antimony is a silvery brittle element primarily derived from stibnite ore usually associated with gold. It is also produced as a by-product of lead-smelting operations. There are two main antimony products marketed, antimony metal and antimony trioxide.

Consumption in the United States (% of Use: 1981)

Flame retardants	55
Transportation (incl. batteries)	15
Ceramics and glass	15
Chemicals	5
Other	10

Uses

The use of antimonial lead in storage batteries, long its most important outlet, is declining with the increased production of maintenance-free lead/tin/calcium vehicle batteries in the United States. From an antimony content in battery alloys of 12 per cent, there has been a decline to the present content levels of between 2.5 per cent and 6 per cent.

Other uses for antimonial lead alloys are in power transmission and communications equipment, ammunition, solder, tank linings, roofing sheets, chemical pumps and pipes and antifriction bearings. The advantages that antimony provides in these uses are that it increases hardness and therefore working life, minimises shrinkage and lowers melting points.

The major use of antimony is in the form of an antimony oxide in flame retardation. Antimony trioxide or trichloride in an organic solvent is extensively used as a flame retardant in carpets, underlays and in the interior trims of automobiles. Trioxide adds hardness and increases the acid resistance of enamel coverings for refrigerators, bathtubs, sinks and toilet bowls.

High quality glass for television screens increasingly contains sodium antimonate, while pentasulphide (Sb_2S_5) is used as a vulcanising agent in the rubber industry. The textile industry uses the trioxide as a finishing additive to filter out the ultraviolet sunlight wavelengths from fibres.

In the paint industry, trioxide is used as a white pigment and with various chemical compounds as black, vermillion, yellow and orange. The infra-red-reflecting characteristics of some pigments make them attractive for use in camouflage paints.

High purity antimony is used in the elctronics industry in the indium-antimony and aluminium-antimony intermetallic alloys used in transistors and rectifiers.

Beryllium (Be)

Beryllium is a steel-grey, hard and light metal rarely seen in its pure form. Beryl is the only major beryllium mineral found in sufficient concentration to constitute an ore mineral. Usually found in the form of crystals in pegmatite dykes, beryl is so erratically distributed in those dykes that extraction for the beryl ore alone is uneconomic and it is produced as a by-product of molybdenum or lithium or of gem-type beryl.

A second source of beryllium is bertrandite, of which the most well-known deposit is in the Spor Mountain area in Utah, USA. The ore there averages less than 1 per cent BeO and the ore is much more finely grained than beryl and it is only a competitive alternative to beryl because it is produced by open-cast mining.

The mineral chrysoberyl ($BeAl_2O_4$), which is found in Alaska's Seward Peninsula, is in small deposits which are not yet economically workable.

Consumption in the United States (% of Use: 1981)

Nuclear reactors and aerospace applications (metal)	40
Electrical equipment (as an alloy)	35
Electronic components	15
Other uses	10

Uses

Only important in industry since the Second World War, beryllium is used as an oxide, a metal and an alloy. The major use is in the form of beryllium metal as an alloy, especially with copper. Beryllium-copper, often referred to as 'super-bronze', is the highest-ranked copper-base alloy in terms of strength, durability and hardness, thermal conductivity, electrical conductivity and corrosion resistance. It is easy to machine and to fabricate, non-magnetic and spark-resistant.

Table 2.1 details some of the uses of beryllium-copper. The two basic compositions of beryllium-copper contain either 0.4 per cent or 1.7 per cent beryllium with cobalt additions. Recent new applications for the alloy are as heavily loaded bushings in low-speed drivers for steel-mill equipment, in housing for submarine cables, as non-sparking components in valves handling flammable liquids, and in tools for use in hazardous environments, in metal casting and plastic moulding tooling and as dual-metal composite strip for two-component electrical connectors.

Rapid growth is expected for the nickel-beryllium alloys that contain up to 2 per cent beryllium and have a strength and hardness almost equalling that of some alloy steels. This alloy is used for high-strength springs operating at up to 260°C, while heavier wrought and cast beryllium parts are being used as tooling in glass and fibreglass forming and as permanent moulds for metal casting.

Beryllium metal has a high melting point and is one of the lightest metals stable in air. In the nuclear field its low absorption and low atomic weight make it suitable as a moderator and a reflector of neutrons in nuclear reactors and as windows in X-ray and radiation-measuring equipment. Gyroscopic guidance systems containing beryllium are used for strategic missiles and for long-range commercial and military aircraft. Further, a fire-control system used on some F-4 aircraft on several earth resources satellites utilises the typical properties and low density of beryllium. The Lockheed C-5 is among the users of beryllium for aircraft disc brakes. Its high melting point and resistance

Table 2.1: Some Uses of Beryllium-copper Alloys

Electrical purposes	
	Spring contacts, connectors and clips
	Switch blades and components
Mechanical engineering	
	Non-sparking tools
	Electrode holders in resistance welders
	Flash buttwelding dies
	Wear-resistance parts (guides, cams, etc.)
	Chains
	Non-magnetic high-strength parts
	Dies for plastics moulding
	Springs
Heat exchangers	
	Bellows and flexible pipes
	Cryogenic tubes and assemblies
Spacecraft	
	Vanguard 3: Beryllium-copper bellows in battery pressure valve
	Ranger 1: Beryllium-copper alloy 25 in gear materials in antenna drive
	Explorer 13: Beryllium-copper pressure cell detectors
	Navigational Satellite 7A: Beryllium-copper strip and spring
	Telstar 1: Beryllium-copper tabs on solar cell module
	Mariner 2: Beryllium-copper alloy in gear materials in antenna drive

to oxidation have led to its use as a fuel canning material. The use of beryllium metal has been restricted to unstressed areas due to the brittleness which it acquires on prolonged exposure to radiation.

Beryllium oxide has its main use in the ceramics industry where its high thermal conductivity and shock resistance and its high electrical resistivity are advantages. Because it conducts heat but not electricity well, it is used as a heat sink and for electrical resistors in small electronic devices. Its high transparency to microwaves has led to its use in windows, helix support rods and microwave device components. Beryllia ceramics are used in laser tubes, electronic ignition systems, high-speed computers, microprocessors, radar and other integrated circuit systems where high temperature resistance is important. A beryllia-cast tape has been developed which can lower the cost of producing integrated circuits.

Cadmium (Cd)

Cadmium is a relatively rare element, discovered as an impurity in pharmaceutical zinc carbonate in Germany in 1817. Greenockite or cadmium sulphide is the only common cadmium mineral; however, it does not occur in sufficient concentration to make the extraction of cadmium economical. Cadmium is recovered primarily from many zinc ores in the extraction and refining process, and also from zinc-bearing lead ores, from complex copper-lead-zinc ores and from the processing of flue dusts and other secondary materials.

Refined cadmium is sold in the form of ingots and sticks with a minimum purity of 99.95 per cent.

World Consumption (Western world) (% of Use: 1980)

Electroplating	40
Pigments	25
Stabilisers	10
Batteries	20
Alloys	5

Consumption in the United States (% of Use: 1981)

Plated hardware	34
Batteries	22
Transportation	17
Pigments	13
Plastics and synthetic products	11
Other	3

Uses

Cadmium's major use is still in the electroplating of iron and steel products to protect them from oxidation. Cadmium-plated parts are used in automobiles, in many household appliances including radios and television sets, in aircraft and in electrical equipment. Electroplating is a less important use in Japan and Europe where stringent environmental legislation has encouraged switching to alternative materials, like zinc plating. Cadmium's better resistance to alkaline and humid atmosphere is reducing the possibility of substitution in the manufacture of defence equipment.

Nickel cadmium rechargeable batteries are the fastest growing use of cadmium, being used to provide power for consumer rechargeable appliances, for hand tools and for computer memories. In the medical market, nickel-cadmium batteries provide the power for prosthetic devices such as artificial limbs and nerve stimulators. Potentially, nickel-cadmium batteries could be made to run forever provided that the separator material and the cell are prevented from deterioration.

Flooded or vented batteries are used almost exclusively to start engines on jet aircraft, due to their superior performance to that of sealed lead-acid batteries. Microprocessor-controlled toys and games are powered by nickel-cadmium batteries – a further recent growth area.

Cadmium is used in the manufacture of pigments and chemicals. For example, cadmium sulphides provide yellow-to-orange colours and cadmium sulphoselenides provide pink-to-red and maroon colours for ceramics and plastics. Cadmium phosphors are used in mono and colour television set tubes. Cadmium stearates are stabilisers in polyvinyl-chloride (PVC) plastic manufacture and cadmium's photochemical properties have led to its use in smoke alarm systems and solar energy cells. Cadmium-based stabilisers are added to PVC and to related polymers to arrest their degradation on exposure to heat and ultra-violet light.

Apart from its use in nickel-cadmium form, other widely used cadmium alloys include cadmium-silver alloys used for high-speed and high-temperature bearings in internal combustion engines; copper-cadmium alloys that have a higher tensile strength than copper wire hard-drawn; and cadmium fusible alloys of bismuth-lead-cadmium, bismuth-tin-cadmium or lead-tin-cadmium, that are suitable for fire-resisting equipment, telephone circuits and electrical fuse wires.
Cadmium-based alloys absorb neutrons as control elements in nuclear reactors.

An advantage of cadmium plating in the aerospace industry has been its prevention of galvanic corrosion between steel and aluminium.

Chromium (Cr)

Chromium is a very hard bluish-white metal element, obtained mainly from chromite or chrome iron ore (ferrous chromite). For each of chromite's three main fields of application – metallurgical, chemical and refractory – a commercial grade is available. A limited interchange-ability exists between the three grades.

Consumption in the United States (% of Use: 1981)

Construction	19
Machinery and equipment	17
Transportation	12
Refractories	12
Other uses	40

The metallurgical industry used 57 per cent, the chemical industry 25 per cent and the refractory industry 18 per cent in the United States in 1981.

Uses

In recent years the introduction of Vacuum Oxygen Decarburisation (VOD) and Argon Oxygen Decarburisation (AOD) processes have brought changes to ferrochrome requirements in the production of stainless steel. The AOD process has resulted in the use of chrome ores with lower chromium contents and a iron Cr:Fe ratio of less than 3:1 can be used. This has meant a decline in the use of high carbon ferrochrome.

In its metallurgical applications, which are mainly the production of ferroalloys, chromium improves the ability to withstand stress at high temperatures, the resistance to corrosion and oxidation and hardening ability chromium ferroalloys are primarily used in the production of stainless and heat-resisting steels. In 1979 Pratt and Whitney developed a new method of making blades for jet aircraft engines using a single crystal of a nickel-chromium superalloy which cut fuel costs by 3 to 4 per cent and which has potentially much wider applications. Chrome-molybdenum rail steels are a recent development that offers a highly wear-resistant alloy capable of long service in rail transport. A new range of nickel-free stainless steels developed by Nippon Metal Industry has more chrome content than the nickel stainless steels.

In the refractory field, chromite is mainly used in the manufacture of refractory bricks, with other uses in mortars and furnace repair. Oxygen blowing converters in the non-ferrous industry are in increasing use and these replace chrome-magnesite bricks with higher magnesite content bricks. Chrome-magnesite bricks are used in the reheating chambers of glass furnaces in the glass industry.

Chromium chemicals are mostly produced from sodium dichromate which is derived directly from chemical grade chromite. They are used in the manufacture of pigments, to harden gelatine, as mordants and dyes for textiles, and as tanning agents for leather.

Cobalt (Co)

In H.C. Hoover's translation of Agricola's *De Re Metallica* he notes that the word 'colbalt' derives from the Greek word for mine, *cobalos*. The use of cobalt salts to provide a blue colour for Egyptian and Babylonian pottery dates recognition of it at least as far back as 1450 BC. The Swedish chemist, Georg Brandt, who first isolated cobalt as a separ-separate metal in 1735, named it *Kobalt*, a derivative of the German word, *Kobold* which refers to mischievous spirits such as gnomes and goblins. The latter term was used by German miners in Saxony and Bohemia to describe certain ores that were alleged to cause sores on their hands and feet. The arsenic content of the ore rather than the cobalt itself was a more likely culprit.

The metal cobalt ranks 34th in the order of prevalence of elements in the earth's crust, comprising 0.0023 per cent. While it is much more prevalent than silver, lead or nickel, it seldom occurs in sufficient quantity to be mined other than as a by-product. Its main occurrences are in association with copper or nickel sulphides, but it has also been mined as a by-product of iron, zinc, lead, silver and uranium. |

Cobalt Consumption in the United States (% of Use: 1981)

Superalloys (mainly for industrial and aircraft gas turbine engines)	40
Magnetic materials (for electrical applications)	15
Metal cutting and mining tool bits	10
Catalysts	12
Driers	12
Other	11

Uses

Cobalt is a component of virtually all permanent magnet materials. The shift of use within that field, from the Alnico (Al-Ni-Co) permanent magnets to stronger rare earth- (samarium and mischmetal) cobalt magnets and to ceramic ferrites, has reduced the total amount of cobalt used. There is a growing demand for rhenium-cobalt permanent magnets for jewellery.

Cobalt base superalloys are important elements in parts for jet engines and in gas turbine components, while in the machinery industry cobalt metal powder is used as a binder or metal matrix in the production of both cemented carbide and tungsten carbide cutting and boring tools. The stellite group of cobalt-based alloys that contain cobalt, tungsten and chromium are used in cutting tools and in coatings. Cobalt comprises 12 to 18 per cent of most nickel-based superalloys and more than 60 per cent of blade and coating alloys.

Cobalt is used in higher speed tool steels and in some abrasion-resistant die steels and cobalt-based alloys are used in medical and dental work where their lightness and compatibility with body tissues and fluids are important advantages. In the form of cobalt oxide, cobalt is an important additive to glass and ceramics especially as it is able to eliminate iron tint in glass and iron colour in porcelain tile and sanitary ware. It is also important as an additive to cattle feeds, salt-licks and fertilisers used for pastures.

Cobalt's other applications include use as intensifiers for light-sensitive printing plates, in the form of cobalt salts as mordants in dyeing textiles and to improve the stability of foam on beer. Cobalt powder is used in the manufacture of tungsten carbide sintered parts and sintered magnets.

There has been a major shift to low-cobalt or cobalt-containing alloys as a result of the high price and supply uncertainty of cobalt.

Columbium (Niobium) (Cb) (Nb)

Columbium is widely distributed and found in many minerals including columbite, columbo-tantalite, pyrochlore, pandaite and others. Pyrochlore and pandaite ores from Brazil and Canada are the major sources. Columbium was discovered in 1801 and niobium in 1944 and it was only later that they were shown to be the same mineral. Although niobium is the name recognised by the International Union of Pure and Applied Chemistry, the term columbium is more often used in commercial practice.

Consumption in the United States (as metal and alloys in fabricated form) (% of Use: 1981)

Construction	31
Oil and gas industries	16
Transportation	32
Machinery	11
Other	10

Uses

Columbium has become important in steel alloying and in superalloys over the past twenty years. Line pipe for oil and gas pipelines is the largest single application of columbium-alloyed steels. Columbium and columbium-vanadium steels are the preferred choice.

Columbium is important as a microalloying element and with the switch to lighter automobiles the microalloyed steel content of US automobiles had risen from 70 lb in 1973 to 200 lb by 1980. The recent development of Cb-phosphoros alloyed steel has considerable application in automobile manufacture including body components.

In both plain carbon steel and high-strength low-alloy (HSLA) steels columbium is an important component. The microalloyed HSLA concrete reinforcing bar is being increasingly used in construction due to its high strength and cost effectiveness.

Relatively pure (99 per cent+) columbium oxide is in growing use, mostly in conversion to high-purity ferrocolumbium and nickel-columbium alloys used in superalloys and HSLA steels. Superalloys for aircraft engines are the most important use of high-purity columbium. The switch from cobalt-based alloys to nickel-based superalloys is increasing the consumption of columbium due to the latter's higher columbium content.

Columbium-using high-alloy steels and superalloys providing protection from corrosion and high temperatures are used in coal gasification and liquefaction processes.

The superior superconductivity of columbium allows the construction of extremely powerful magnets and has potential for superconductor machines and devices. Very high purity columbium oxide is used in optical glass to give a high refractive index which is important in eyeglass lenses as well as in lenses for cameras, copying machines and scientific equipment.

Germanium (Ge)

Germanium is a brittle, silver-grey metallic chemical element with properties between those of silicon and tin. Although widely distributed in the earth's crust it does not occur in sufficient quantity to justify extraction by itself. The most important commercial source is as a minor by-product of certain zinc ores. It occurs also in silver-tin sulphides and lead-zinc-copper sulphide ores. The copper-zinc ores of Zaire contain germanium in the mineral renierite. There is potentially a large supply of germanium recoverable from the ash and flue dusts resulting from the combustion of coal in power generation.

Consumption in the United States (% of Use: 1981)

Instruments and optical industry	66
Electronic and electrical applications	29
Other	5

Uses

The invention of the transistor in 1948 had a dramatic effect on the demand for germanium, because it was first made of germanium. The year 1966 saw peak use of germanium diodes and transistors due to the increasing use of discrete silicon devices and integrated circuits. The development of hyper-pure silicon reduced the use of germanium not only in transistors but also in other semiconductor devices used in electronic circuitry.

In the late 1970s germanium's use in infra-red systems became of increasing importance with the development of infra-red optics. Germanium is used in the form of optical-grade metal for reflectors which are able to reflect 98 per cent of the available infra-red heat. It offers the other advantages of easy machinability, good mechanical strength and atmospheric inertness.

Germanium dioxide is used for polyester fibre catalysis and use of glass fibres containing a high index germania core has been demonstrated in long-distance telecommunications. In 1978 it was discovered that the addition of lead germanate to the barium titanate used for ceramic capacitors allowed silver to replace palladium conductors and thus simplified manufacture. Germanium dioxide is increasingly used in optical fibres, an important development in telecommunications.

The gamma-ray detector market for germanium has been expanding, although only a small amount of germanium is used; a little germanium is also used in alloying.

Hafnium (Hf)

Hafnium is a metallic element discovered in 1923 and given the Latin name of Copenhagen where the discovery was made. It is present in zirconium minerals found in beach sands and river gravels, and is recovered as a by-product in the production of hafnium-free nuclear-grade zirconium-based alloys. Zircon metal contains about 1 per cent hafnium. Hafnium is recovered as sponge, crystal bar, ingot and recycled scrap.

Consumption in the United States (% of Use: 1981)

Control rods for naval nuclear reactors	50
Ceramics, refractory applications, alloys and carbide in cutting tool alloys	50

Uses

The major use of hafnium is in control rods in nuclear reactors and it is the only material specified for use in nuclear reactors for submarines. It is used as hafnium-columbium carbide in carbide coatings for tool bits as a replacement for tantalum and also as a cladding material. It is important as a refractory metal alloy in high-temperature use as hafnium carbide is the most refractory binder known. Hafnium has high hot water corrosion resistance, good ductility and machinability. It is a successful insulator for separation and electrical insulating in thermocouples, and is used in high-temperature superalloys for jet engines.

Indium (In)

Indium occurs in small quantities in a number of lead zinc ores and in some tin, tungsten, manganese, lead and copper ores. The present supply is obtained mainly as a minor by-product of lead and zinc smelting and refining.

Consumption in the United States (% of Use: 1981)

Electrical and electronic components	40
Solders, alloys and coatings	40
Research and other uses	20

Uses

Indium is important in the nuclear industry in the making of control rods for the batteries in atomic reactors where its low melting point and high sensitivity to temperature changes are important; but its main demand has come from other uses in the past few years. In the electronics industry indium is used in high-grade electronic contacts and in semiconductors, printed circuits are printed with indium-based alloys and indium-containing solders are used in electronics and cryogenics.

Copper-lead indium bearings are used in sports cars and in conveyor belts and indium is used in sodium discharge lamps as a fusible alloy in dentistry and other industries and as a doping agent for germanium semiconductors.

A recent use of growing importance is as a transparent, electrically conductive coating on glass for liquid-crystal displays on watches and calculators. In the solar energy field indium is one of a number of metals being evaluated for use in solar cells.

Lithium (Li)

The lightest of all solid elements, lithium is a soft very reactive metallic element. Lithium mineral concentrate is produced from the mining and beneficiation of pegmatite ores. Spodumene concentrate is the major source, with lithium chloride, lepidolite and petalite concentrates the other sources. The commercial mining of lithium minerals dates from 1898 when spodumene was produced in South Dakota in the United States.

Consumption in the United States (% of Use: 1981)

Aluminium potlines	33
Glass and ceramics and lubrication	40
Other	27

Uses

Lithium, which is a very active electrochemical material, provides more energy in a smaller space as anode material for batteries than other materials. General Electric is marketing lithium/manganese dioxide batteries and it is expected that 3V lithium batteries, which are thinner than alternatives, will have an expanding market. In addition to thinness lithium batteries have a very long shelf life and a longer working life than other batteries. Work is proceeding on the development of rechargeable lithium batteries and, in the meantime, military applications, heart pacemakers, watches and calculators offer a growing market for the lithium batteries provided by existing technology. In 1982, Eastman Kodak introduced a lithium-powered 'disc' camera.

Lithium carbonate has increasing use in the aluminium industry where it offers the advantages of reducing fluoride emissions and improving the conductivity of the fused electrolyte. The US Bureau of Mines reports that the largest end use of lithium is in aluminium potlines.

Other industries utilise lithium products: the synthetic rubber industry used butyllithium; lithium hydroxide is used in multipurpose greases; and the ceramics industry uses lithium ores and lithium carbonate for enamels, glazes and coatings.

Manganese (Mn)

Regarded as a variety of iron for many centuries, manganese was first recognised as an element in 1774 by a Swedish chemist Scheele and isolated in the same year by Gahn. It is a silver-white brittle metallic element. The most important manganese ore minerals are oxides. Pyrolusite, a mineral form of manganese dioxide, is a common manganese oxide mineral and rhodochrosite is the principal specific manganese carbonate ore mineral.

Manganese Consumption in the United States (% of Use: 1981)

Transportation	20
Construction	23
Machinery	16
Other	41

Uses

Almost all manganese produced is consumed by the iron and steel industry. Manganese combines with sulphur to produce a manganese sulphide slag easily separated from steel and it is as a desulphuriser and as a deoxidiser that it has its most important and irreplaceable use. However, the shift away from the basic Bessemer steelmaking processes towards the electric, basic oxygen and Q Bo P type of process has reduced average manganese consumption per tonne of steel produced from 10.4 kg when only the Bessemer process was used to the present estimate of 6.5 kg. Manganese adds strength and hardness to aluminium, is alloyed with copper to form manganese bronzes and adds hardness and corrosion resistance to magnesium.

Manganese dioxides are of critical importance in the production of dry-cell batteries and have further uses in the production of hydroquinone (which is used in photographic developers and in the production of rubbers and plastics), in the leaching of uranium ores and in the electrolytic production of zinc.

Manganese in the forms of manganese sulphate or manganous oxide is an additive to animal and poultry feeds and to fertilisers and manganese-deficient soils.

Mercury (Hg)

Mercury, or quicksilver, described by Aristotle in the fourth century BC, is mainly derived from the red sulphide ore, cinnabar. It is the only metal that is liquid at normal temperatures, becoming a white solid below its melting point of – 38.85 C and a colourless vapour above its boiling point of 357.25 C. The product of mercury mines, cinnabar ore, is processed to recover prime virgin metal usually more than 99.9 per cent pure which is sold in flasks containing 76 1b.

Mercury Consumption in the United States (% of Use: 1981)

Electrical apparatus	56
Electrolytic preparation of chlorine and caustic soda	13
Mildew-proofing paint	14
Industrial and control instruments	10
Other	7

Uses

Environmental considerations reduced several major end uses for mercury to virtually nil in the mid-1970s. The use of mercury in insecticides was phased out and caustic soda plants replaced mercury cells by diaphragm cells (although electricity use was drastically increased by that substitution) and organotin compounds were substituted for mercury in the paint industry.

Major uses of mercury are in the manufacture of electrical apparatus, including mercury lamps, batteries, rectifier bulbs, oscillators and switches. There is a preference for the use of mercury lamps over incandescent lamps for street lighting and industrial purposes, due to the greater adaptability of the mercury lamps to higher voltage supply.

Still a major, though declining, use is in the electrolytic preparation of chlorine and caustic soda, but in this application as well as in its uses in mildew-proofing paints, industrial and control instruments, pharmaceuticals, insecticides and fungicides, mercury is restricted in its use or even entirely banned by some governments.

The chloride, oxide and sulphate mercury compounds are good catalysts for a number of chemical reactions, including those involved in the making of plastics. Mercury can be used as a shield against atomic radiation because of its capacity to absorb neutrons.

Molybdenum (Mo)

Molybdenum is a silver-white metallic element used mainly in the form of molybdic oxide or ferromolybdenum as an alloying agent in steel, cast iron and superalloys. It enhances the ability to harden, and provides strength, toughness, wear and corrosion resistance. Known at least since Greek and Roman times but often confused with other minerals of similar characteristics such as graphite, molybdenite was shown by the Swedish chemist, Kaal Scheele, to be a discrete mineral sulphide in 1778. In 1782 another Swede, P.J. Hjelm produced an impure powder of the molybdenite metal by using charcoal heat to reduce the element's acid-forming oxide. In 1893 German chemists reduced calcium molybdate to 96 per cent pure molybdenum.

Mainly recovered from low-grade deposits of the mineral molybdenite (MoS_2) molybdenum is also obtained as a by-product from mining large low-grade porphyry copper deposits.

Molybdenum Consumption in the United States (% of Use: 1981)

Machinery	34
Transportation	17
Oil and gas industry	20
Chemicals	13
Electrical	8
Other	8

Major Processed Forms

Molybdenum Disulphide. These are purified molybdenite concentrates used in the manufacture of lubricants.

Molybdic Oxide (MoO_3). The most important grade of molybdic oxide is technical grade molybdic oxide (TMO) which is sold as powder and as briquettes (the latter have pitch as a binding component). Pure molybdic oxide (with at least 99.5 per cent $Mo0_3$) is the other grade of molybdic oxide produced. When molybdenum concentrates are roasted to form molybdic oxide, sulphur dioxide is released into the atmosphere creating a pollution problem.

Ferromolybdenum. This is an alloy of molybdenum and iron with a molybdenum content ranging from 58 to 64 per cent.

Molybdates. This take three forms: ammonium, sodium and calcium molybdates.

Molybdenum Metal. A powder is first produced by reducing ammonium molybdate or pure molybdic oxide with hydrogen and the powder is then pressed into small ingots or cast into large ingots of molybdenum metal.

Uses

Technical grade molybdic oxide and ferromolybdenum added to steel melts to produce molybdenum-containing steels are the major uses of molybdenum. Molybdenum is added to alloy steels that are used in the production of transport equipment, industrial machinery and tools. The recent development of dual phase steels in which molybdenum provides increased strength and ductility, allows automobile manufacturers to reduce the thickness and weight of components formerly produced from carbon steel. A further recently introduced product is chrome-molybdenum rail steels, that provide high wear-resistance, and have a useful role to play in rail transport.

The strength, toughness, heat and corrosion resistance of molybdenum-containing alloys has led to their use in the casing, tubing and drill pipe used for oil and gas wells. In oil refineries themselves, molybdenum-containing catalysts are used. A switch to synthetic fuels would not reduce the demand for molybdenum because of its use for pressure vessels in synthetic fuel plants and its use as a catalyst in coal liquifaction. Japan in particular, is using 18 Cr-2 Mo ferrite stainless steel in solar collection.

In many superalloys, including the nickel-based and cobalt-based forms, molybdenum improves high-temperature strength or the corrosion resistance. It is used in the high-temperature superalloys for military aircraft and new commercial aircraft. The eutectic superalloys used in turbine-blades for higher-thrust engines have a molybdenum content of between 18 per cent and 37 per cent.

Among its newer uses molybdenum is important in pollution control, for example US pulp and paper plants meeting the Federal requirements on effluents have had to upgrade their steels to higher molybdenum levels; and Canada's Teck Corporation is developing a new lithium-molybdenum disulphide battery.

Nickel (Ni)

Nickel is a silver-coloured metal that is mainly derived from sulphide deposits. In addition to nickel-copper sulphides, nickel silicates and nickel laterites and serpentines are also sources. Nickel sulphides are usually associated with copper and iron sulphides and the deposits often contain cobalt, silver, gold, the platinum group metals, selenium and tellurium.

Consumption in the United States (% of Use: 1981)

Transportation	25
Chemical industry	15
Electrical equipment	15
Construction	10
Fabricated metal products	10
Other	25

The US Bureau of Mines noted that 45 per cent of nickel consumption occurred in the production of stainless and alloy steel; 30 per cent in nonferrous alloys; and 15 per cent in electroplating.

Uses

Over 90 per cent of nickel's use is in alloys with other metals. Although there has been some substitution in the stainless steel sector, which is the most important consumer, the proportion of nickel used has remained fairly constant for more than three decades now. Stainless steel is used in the construction of aircraft, trucks, automobiles and railway trucks as well as in household appliances.

Nickel/chromium plating has long been an important market and recent developments in electroforming promise continued growth. Among the high alloys materials being used for corrosive oilfield service, nickel alloys and austenitic steels containing nickel are important.

Superalloys, which have a nickel content of over 50 per cent, are alloys used in high-temperature applications in aircraft and spacecraft including gas turbines and jet engines. In addition to their high-temperature strength, they offer resistance to corrosion and oxidation.

Nickel is used in a wide range of alloys which have extensive uses. For example, Nickel silver is used for spring contacts in telecommunications and electrical equipment; for deep-drawn items, pressing and springs in mechanical engineering applications; and in cylinder lock keys and key blanks, finger plates, base metal for plating or enamelling, zip fasteners, tableware, candelabra, trays, watch-cases and costume jewellery. Cupronickel or copper-nickel alloys are used in the electrical industry in resistors, radar waveguides, and leads, wires and switches; in munitions for shell-driving blanks and cartridge cases and in desalination equipment, heat exchangers condensers, piping for brines and sea-water.

New markets that offer potential for further use of nickel are electric-powered vehicles and solar collector panels and solar power plants in the solar energy industry. Nickel-cadmium batteries are already in use and General Motors Corporation has developed a zinc-nickel oxide battery which offers more than double the energy storage capacity of lead-acid batteries.

Platinum Group Metals

The platinum group metals (PGMs), often referred to as noble or precious metals, consist of six closely related metals that commonly occur together in nature, though in varying proportions. It is usual to consider the six metals as comprising two groups: the heavy or high density group of platinum, iridium and osmium; and the lighter group of palladium, rhodium and ruthenium. These metals are usually by-products of nickel-copper mining.

Consumption in the United States (% of Use: 1981)

Automotive (mainly as catalysts)	30
Electrical	26
Chemical (mainly as catalysts)	14
Dental	12
Other	18

Consumption of Individual Platinum Group Metals in the United States, 1980 (troy oz)

Platinum (Pt)

Automotive	517,143
Chemical	118,956
Petroleum	144,039
Glass	52,897
Electrical	150,060
Dental and medical	25,831
Jewellery and decoration	50,998

Miscellaneous	58,307
Total	1,118,231
Iridium (Ir)	
Chemical	4,134
Electrical	11,273
Jewellery and decoration	3,092
Dental and medical	495
Glass	50
Petroleum	4,058
Miscellaneous	482
Total	23,584
Osmium (Os)	
Dental and medical	498
Chemical	321
Total	819
Palladium (Pd)	
Automotive	176,518
Electrical	312,778
Chemical	119,905
Dental and medical	244,279
Petroleum	22,013
Jewellery and decoration	13,491
Glass	1,155
Miscellaneous	21,828
Total	911,967
Rhodium (Rh)	
Automotive	37,012
Chemical	5,273
Glass	8,581
Jewellery and decoration	5,434
Electrical	14,818
Petroleum	662
Dental and medical	45
Miscellaneous	1,703
Total	73,528

Ruthenium (Ru)

Electrical	37.224
Chemical	35,972
Jewellery and decoration	560
Automotive	674
Dental and medical	508
Miscellaneous	2,843
Total	77,781

Uses

A major new use for platinum and palladium has been in catalytic converters for the control of automotive exhaust emissions. The automotive emission standards of the United States' Environmental Protection Agency and of the Japanese government are best satisfied by the use of these two metals as catalysts in converters and the more stringent standards established for the 1980 and later model-years involve increased metal loadings in catalytic converters. In order to control nitrogen oxide emissions, however, it appears that rhodium will need to be added but the only rhodium-type converter so far developed requires too much rhodium for the supply of the metal to meet the requirements if this converter was universally adopted.

A platinum-rhenium catalyst is used in the reforming of petroleum for the production of low-lead and lead-free high-octane gasolines and this use has become of greater importance with the restriction placed by the United States EPA in 1979 on the use of lead as a petrol additive.

In the electrical industry platinum's main uses are in electrical contacts for which it provides long-lasting low contact resistance and good thermal stability, and in electrodes where it provides protection against corrosion. Platinum's uses in the electronic industry are in printed circuits, and in electrical furnaces as well as in thermocouples and electric contacts for telephone equipment, and platinum-gold-silver are used in low-voltage contacts.

In the chemical industry platinum and platinum alloys are widely used in both laboratory and process equipment to provide linings and other protection from corrosion. Platinum-lined vessels are also used in the glass industry to prevent the contamination of optical glass by metallic oxides. Platinum is particularly important in the nitric acid industry where it is used as gauze for the oxidation of ammonia, usually when alloyed with 10 per cent rhodium. Platinum bushings, again with 10 per cent rhodium, are used in glass-fibre production.

Various platinum alloys are used in spinnerettes for the production of viscose rayon and platinum-cobalt alloys (50 per cent cobalt) forms very powerful magnets which are malleable and ductile before hardening.

In Japan, but not so far in other countries,the jewellery industry is the major consumer of platinum metals.

It is thought that platinum may be important in the catalytic electrodes of fuel cells which are directly to convert fuel into electricity.

Palladium's good heat and corrosion resistance has led to its use for low-voltage, low-current electrical relays and, in conjunction with silver and copper, it is used as a high-quality brazing alloy in jet engines and in special purpose valves. As an addition to stainless steel or titanium, palladium increases passivity and enhances the resistance of special steels to sulphuric acid corrosion. Although the demand for palladium-bearing prosthodontic and orthodontic devices in dentistry may decline with the increased emphasis on preventive dental care, palladium load-bearing devices for the replacement of damaged or arthritic bones and joints are expected to be in increased demand.

Rhodium's main use is as an alloy with platinum to increase strength and higher temperature resistance. Pure rhodium is used as a catalyst fo acetic acid production, for the plating of jewellery and of electrical parts and in electric furnace windings where the high temperatures prevent the use of platinum.

Iridium, said to be the most corrosion-resistant of all metals, is mostly used as a 30 per cent component of iridium-platinum alloys. Its main use is for hardening and it is used in spark plugs for aircraft to resist lead corrosion. Ruthenium is used in a 30 per cent platinum 70 per cent wear-resistant alloy and otherwise mainly as a hardener for platinum or palladium. Osmium is the hardest of the platinum group metals to work and is only used in the production of the very hard tips for fountain-pen nibs, record needles, electric contacts and instrument pivots.

Rhenium (Re)

Rhenium is derived mainly from molybdenite recovered from porphyry ores, although it was first produced in the 1930s in Germany from potash and copper-smelter residues. Rhenium is volatised as rhenium leptoxide and concentrated in flue dusts and stackgases in the roasting of rhenium-bearing molybdenite concentrate to produce molybdenum trioxide.

Consumption in the United States (% of Use: 1981)

Catalysts in low-lead and lead-free gasoline	92
Other (including thermocouples, heating elements, X-ray tubes and targets, flash bulbs, vacuum tubes, electrical contacts and metallic coatings	8

Uses

Since 1969 the dominant use of rhenium has been in bimetallic platinum-rhenium catalysts used in petroleum refining to produce low-lead and lead-free high-octane gasoline. In 1979, with the US restriction on the use of lead as a petrol additive, this application became even more important. Substitutes for rhenium in this area are continually being evaluated.

Other uses of rhenium are mainly in alloys with tungsten and molybdenum among other metals, for heating elements, X-ray tubes and targets, flash bulbs, metallic coatings and contact points, thermocouples and vacuum tubes.

The US Bureau of Mines suggests that the high density, high modulus of elasticity and high melting point of rhenium are properties that make its use in a wide range of applications of considerable potential. Jet-engine turbine blades, and heat and radiation shields for nuclear and missile applications are mentioned as potential uses.

Selenium (Se)

Selenium is a non-metallic element that occurs in minerals associated with copper, lead and iron sulphides. It was discovered by J. J. Berzelius, a Swedish chemist, in 1817 in the red residue found in sulphuric acid prepared as part of a pyrite mining operation. It is named after the Greek goddess of the moon, Selene. It is recovered commercially from electrolytic copper refinery slimes and from flue dusts from copper and lead smelters. Recycling of selenium from its xerographic uses has become an important source of supply. Selenium occurs in coal deposits but recovery of it from this source is considered to be unlikely.

Selenium is marketed in two grades: commercial selenium which has a minimum content of 0.995 Se; and high purity selenium which has a minimum of 0.999 Se. It is also marketed in the forms of ferroselenium, selenium dioxide, barium selenite, nickel-selenium, sodium selenate and sodium selenite and zinc selenite.

Consumption in the United States (% of Use: 1981)

Electronic and photocopier components	35
Glass manufacturing	30
Chemicals and pigments	25
Other	10

Uses

The glassmaking industry, in which selenium had its first commercial use, is still a major user for glass decolourising and tinting. Selenium provides the brilliant red colour used in traffic lights and other signal lenses. There is concern about selenium emissions and recovery, in particular due to the listing of selenium sulphide in the Occupational Safety and Health Administration's list of potential chemical carcinogens. At the same time, however, conservationists favour a shift from petroleum-based plastic containers to glass containers which may increase the use of selenium. Selenium-tinted windows which reduce heat conductivity are expected to be in growing demand.

In the pigment industry, selenium is one of the inorganic-base pigments used to prevent fading due to heat, light and chemical exposure in high-temperature cured plastics, as well as in ceramics, paints, enamels and inks. As a trace element selenium prevents white muscle disease in livestock and poultry and it is used with US Food and Drug Administration approval as a nutrient in beef and dairy-cattle feeds and it is proposed that it also be added to poultry and swine feed.

An historically important but now declining use for selenium is in the production of rectifiers used in electroplating, welding and battery-charging. Selenium-lead battery alloys have increasing use and selenium is expected to be an essential component in maintenance-free batteries.

The addition of 0.2 to 0.35 per cent selenium improves the machinability of stainless steel with no reduction in its corrosion-resistance and the addition of smaller amounts of selenium is able to improve the forging characteristics of steel. Metallurgical applications represent only about 5 per cent of the use of selenium. A minor amount of selenium is used in the manufacture of delay-action blasting caps.

In the rubber industry finely ground elemental selenium and selenac (selenium dialkyldithio-carbamate) increase the vulcanisation rate of natural and synthetic rubber and improve the ageing and mechanical properties of both sulphurless and low-sulphur rubber.

Selenium is used in the production of cortisone and nicotine acids and in a number of medications and shampoos used to control dermatitis in humans and animals, as well as in insecticides and herbicides.

The major market and the one offering the most growth at present is xerography, in particular plain-paper copiers. Organic-based substitutes for the selenium photo-receptor have been developed, but selenium is well placed in both present and future technological developments in the photocopier field. This market is also a major source of scrap for recycling.

New uses being investigated for selenium include its possible use in the photogalvanic cells that convert light energy to electrical energy.

Tantalum (Ta)

Tantalum is a scarce bluish metallic element that is chemically related to vanadium and niobium (columbium) and is usually associated with niobium in nature. Tantalite or tantalite-columbite is the main source of tantalum, but it is usually produced as a co-product or a by-product of tin mining and only rarely independently.

Tantalum Consumption in the United States (% of Use: 1981)

Electronic components	73
Machinery	19
Transportation	6
Other	2

Uses

Approximately two-thirds of tantalum production is used in capacitors for military applications and in the communications, data processing and consumer electronics industries. Capacitors for miniaturised electronic systems and for usage at extreme temperatures are regarded as strong growth areas. Another use of tantalum in the electronics industry is as rectifiers, oscillators, timing devices, control equipment, alarms and signals. It is used as an absorber of residual gases in some electronic tubes.

A further important use has been as a carbide in the tips of cutting tools, but there has been a significant and permanent replacement in the form of cemented carbides and the use of coated inserts in these is reducing the use of tantalum still further.

A new and growing use for tantalum is expected in the aerospace industry following Pratt and Whitney's choice of a nickel-base superalloy with a 12 per cent tantalum content, for use in turbine blades in engines. Tantalum's use in high-temperature alloys and mill products is also growing, in particular it imparts a heat resistance to superalloys used in turbine engines that enables them to run at high temperatures and gain increased fuel efficiency.

Tellurium (Te)

Tellurium is one of the most scarce of elements, primarily recovered commercially from the precious-metal-rich anode slimes obtained from the electrolytic refining of copper. Lead ore contains about a quarter of the tellurium content of copper ore. The US Geological Survey has estimated that an average tellurium content of four times that of economic copper deposits is contained in coal deposits. The mining of oceanic manganese nodules is a potential future source of by-product tellurium.

Tellurium is sold in commercial grade powder and slab form and as tellurium oxide.

Tellurium Consumption in the United States (% of Use: 1981)

Iron and steel products	65
Nonferrous metals	20
Chenicals	10
Other	5

Uses

In the metallurgical industry tellurium is used as a carbonide stabiliser in the production of malleable iron castings, as a chilled white iron surface and as a freemachining agent in steel and copper alloys and in low-carbon sulphurised steels and stainless steels. Tellurium is important as a catalyst used as a hardening agent in synthetic rubbers and as a chilling agent for malleable cast iron. It is both a curing agent and accelerator in rubber compounding and is a catalyst for synthetic fibre and ethylene glycol production.

Bismuth and lead tellurides and their alloys are used as semi-conductors in infra-red detectors and photoelectric cells among other uses. Experimental uses of tellurium include as a high-absorption-collector surface film for solar heat collector panels where it reduces re-emission of solar energy and in thermonuclear heart pacemakers in which a tellurium alloy converts nuclear-power-derived heat to electrical energy.

Titanium (Ti)

The ninth most abundant element in the earth's crust, titanium is a light, hard, corrosion-resistant silver-white metal. It is known to occur in at least 47 different mineral species; however, rutile and ilmenite are commercially the most important. Rutile (TiO_2) contains 60 per cent titanium and ilmenite ($FeTiO_3$) contains 31.6 per cent titanium. Ilmenite occurs as mineable deposits in rock (often in association with iron ore) and as sand deposits. Although rutile is present in most rocks it is rarely sufficiently concentrated there to be mineable. The most important rutile deposits are in beach sand.

Titanium Dioxide Pigment Consumption in the United States (% of Use: 1981)

Paints	47
Paper products	26
Plastics and synthetics	11
Rubber products	2
Ceramics and glass	2
Other	12

Titanium Metal Consumption in the United States (% of Use: 1981)

Aerospace and jet engines	60
Industrial equipment	20
Steel and other alloys	20

Uses

The major use of titanium metal is in jet engines, airframes, space and missile applications. A majority of new civilian and military aircraft built since the early 1950s have contained titanium or titanium-alloy components and the new generation of Boeings and advanced strategic air-launched missiles will all contain titanium alloys. Boeing is using Ti-10V-2Fe-3Al forgings for the 757 aircraft; Ti-6Al-2Sn-4Zr-2Mo-0.1Si is the baseline alloy for the airframe and control surface structures for the next generation of advance strategic air-launched missiles and for the mixer for Pratt and Whitney's JT8-209 engine for McDonnell Douglas's new DC9-80. In 1968, the 666 commercial jet liners manufactured in the USA used 3,400 tons of titanium; the 389 jet liners delivered in 1981 required 6,400 tons.

It is the pursuit of better fuel economy and lower noise that has led to the replacement of nickel alloys by titanium in these uses; however, a high energy consumption is required in its production and for this latter reason its application in US military aircraft has been reduced. For example the F-14 contains 25 per cent titanium and the F-15, 35 per cent, but the more recent F-18 has 12 per cent and the F-16 2 per cent.

Titanium's outstanding corrosion resistance has led to its use as a cathode in the electrolytic extraction of metals in particular copper, nickel and gold, as well as in the metal-finishing and chemical-plant construction industries. Its resistance to wet chlorine has allowed it to replace glass in heat-exchange equipment and in chloride-processing plant, and titanium is also used in nitric acid manufacture and fertiliser production.

Marine uses of titanium are widespread due to the metal's resistance to attack by saline and polluted cooling waters. Major marine uses are in weight-critical structures like hydrofoils, off-shore oil rigs and in titanium condenser tubes and underwater craft construction while the use of titanium in multi-stage flash desalination plants is a potentially large application.

Titanium and its alloys are important in the manufacture of surgical implants not only because of the metal's resistance to corrosion but also because of its combination of strength, lightness and ability to be fabricated in intricate forms. A new family of hardsurfacing powders containing titanium carbide, now being evaluated, offer better abrasion and erosion resistance than other materials.

Titanium dioxide pigments, the second of the main forms in which tianium is utilised, offer the advantages of resistance to chemical attack, thermal stability non-toxicity and opacity. Paints, varnishes and lacquers are the major uses, with the paper industry using almost a quarter of production; plastics, rubber, textiles, floor-coatings, ceramics and inks are the other manufacturing uses.

Tungsten (W)

Tungsten is a hard, brittle metallic element which was discovered and isolated from its ore minerals, scheelite and wolframite, in the 1780s. It is found on almost all continents, occurring as Wo3 in the minerals scheelite, ferberite, huebnerite and wolframite.

Tungsten Consumption in the United States (% of Use: 1981

Metalworking and construction machinery	78
Transportation	9

Lamps and lighting	6
Electrical	4
Other	3

Uses

Tungsten carbide (WC), one of the hardest materials known, is used in the cutting edges of machine tools, including drill bits. Recently improvements have been made in the efficiency of tungsten use including the introduction of indexable inserts for cutting tools. These make more cutting edges per unit volume available and facilitate recycling. The inserts have reduced by half the amount of tungsten carbide used for a given volume of metal cutting. The introduction of coated hardmetals for use in cutting tools involves a thin coating of a diffusion-wear resistant material, like titanium carbo-nitride or alumina, being applied to a substrate of a hardmetal based on tungsten carbide and this increases tool life by three to five times. Major uses for tungsten carbide are cutting and machine tools, punches and dies for metal forming, and bits and tools for drilling equipment.

In alloys, tungsten's main use is in the production of high-speed steels, while superalloys containing tungsten are important in high-temperature uses in highly corrosive environments, for example, for gas turbines. Stellite alloys (nickel-cobalt-chromium-tungsten) are used for high-speed cutting tools and wear-resistant parts. Pure tungsten powder, which is the form in which tungsten is added to alloys, is also used to manufacture ductile tungsten wire for filaments for electric light bulbs.

Tungsten mill products are important in the electrical industries as rods, wire products and electrical contact discs, because of the high melting point, hardness and good electrical conductivity of tungsten. Tungsten wire is used to form cathodes for electron tubes and light bulbs.

Chemicals derived from tungsten are used in textile dyes, inks, paints, enamels and glass. For example, yellow tungsten trioxide is used in oil and water colours, and luminescent tungsten-derived phosphors are used in luminescent pigments, X-ray screens, television picture tubes and fluorescent lights. Tungsten compounds are also used to prepare solid lubricants, lasers and catalysts, chemical reagents and corrosion inhibitors.

Tungsten is also regarded as important in a number of military applications including armour-piercing projectiles, flake sprays, crucibles for reclaiming nuclear fuel, rocket nozzles and heating elements. The military consumption of tungsten is, however, seriously threatened by the successful tests of bullets made from U-238, depleted uranium (D4).

Vanadium (V)

In 1831 a Swedish chemist, Nils Sefström, rediscovered a metal known since 1801 but erroneously classified as an impure base lead chromate in Swedish iron ore samples, which he named vanadium after Freya Vanadis, the Scandinavian goddess of beauty. It was a material used for the locks in the Panama Canal, in the Model T-Ford and for the engine of the Spirit of St Louis.

Although it is a common element in the earth's crust, it does not often occur in a form from which the metal can be economically extracted, and its very high reactivity makes it difficult to isolate as a metal. Early sources of its supply were the lead/zinc ores of South Africa and Rhodesia, while its main sources today are titanium-bearing magnetites, sometimes a co-product with iron, and it is also produced as a uranium by-product and as a by-product of ferrophosphorus. Vanadium in oil is a potentially large source from Central American oilfields. The Flexicoking process recovers 6 per cent vanadium from petroleum ash.

Vanadium Consumption in the United States (% of Use: 1981)

Transportation	35
Construction	27
Machinery	25
Chemicals	4
Others	9

Uses

The major use of vanadium is as a constituent of high-strength, low-alloy (HLSA) steels. The first HLSA steels were developed in Germany during the Second World War when vanadium was exploited as an alternative to scarcer elements like manganese and chromium. HLSA steel is used for pipe fittings and heavy structures. In the early 1970s the development of the controlled-rolling process led to a new type of steel containing 0·05-0·09 per cent vanadium which had a lower carbon content and better weldability. This steel is the most common now used for X65 grades of line pipe and in plate and section uses where high strength, toughness and weldability are important. Italsider, working with the vanadium industry, upgraded this steel in 1974 to X70 for pipes. This vanadium control-rolled steel with niobium is the construction material for one of the world's largest pipelines, the 1,328 km long, 106.7 mm diameter Northern Border Pipeline which is to connect the Alaskan Highway Pipeline at the Alberta border with the USA to a point south-west of Chicago. More than 500 tonnes of vanadium are being used by the eight pipemakers employed in the project.

There is increasing demand for HLSA steels because of their ability to save weight without any reduction in strength. In HLSA and full alloy steels vanadium is added usually in the form of ferrovanadium or proprietary vanadium carbides or carbontrides. Vanadium is an essential element in high-speed tool steels. It has application in a number of titanium-based alloys; for example it was used in two recently developed titanium alloys. The first, the Ti-10V-2Fe-3Al forging alloy, which has high toughness at high strength levels is being evaluated at Boeing and its supporting forging suppliers for use in the new family of Boeing commercial airliners. Its advantage there is in its substantial weight saving compared to steel at high heat levels. The second is the Ti-15V-3Cr-3Al-3Sn strip and sheet alloy. Potential markets for this alloy include high strength brazed honeycomb and for cold formed or welded parts in a number of aerospace applications.

Belli *et al.* (1981) have recently demonstrated that the addition of vanadium or vanadium plus titanium to Fe-Cr-Co hard permanent magnetic alloys retards their brittleness and makes the processing more convenient without changing the magnetic properties. This is important because these alloys otherwise lose their ductility after they are aged to acquire good magnetic properties. It was also reported in early 1981 that the addition of 0.45 per cent vanadium to a 0.06 per cent carbon-manganese steel induces hardenability and this vanadium structural steel has potential for the development of weldable pipeline steel suitable for X70 or X80 grades.

Vanadium has long been used as a catalyst in sulphuric acid production and in controlling sulphur emissions from power plants and chemical plants; however, the quantity consumed is small and is usually recycled for reuse.

The Vanadium International Technical Committee (VANITEC) is sponsoring research and development of new uses of vanadium. Among developments being evaluated is a new steel with 0.45 per cent vanadium for use in the production of heavy-walled line pipe.

Zirconium (Zr)

Zirconium is derived almost entirely from the minerals zircon and baddeleyite. Eudialyte is a possible source. Zircon, the main source, usually contains some 49 per cent zirconium and 0.4 to 1.5 per cent hafnium. Baddeleyite, which is less common, contains up to 73 per cent zirconium and 0.4 to 1.7 per cent hafnium. Zirconium is a quite common element, listed 20th in order of abundance in the earth's crust.

World Consumption (% of End Use: 1981 est.)

Refractory	34
Foundry	31
Ceramic	26
Other	9

Consumption in the United States (% of End Use: 1981 est.)

Foundry	40
Refractory	17
Ceramic	13
Abrasives	4
Chemicals	3
Other	23

Uses

Zirconium has only been produced commercially since the early 1950s Zircon sand and flour is a raw material for zirconium metal, alloys and chemicals, and is used in foundries, refractories and ceramics. Zircon is in growing demand as a high, quality, long-life refractory material for linings and there has been a shift from the use of chromite to the use of zircon in foundries.

Zirconia or zirconium dioxide, which is produced by chemical or furnace treating of zircon sand, is the highest temperature oxide in commercial use. Among its uses are electronic ceramics and ceramic colours, abrasive polishing compounds, zirconium metal and high-temperature refractories. Zircon concentrates are used in the foundry industry, ferrozirconium is used in the steel industry and zirconium alloys.

A technique has been developed for producing glass-reinforced cement products using an alkali-resistant glass fibre that contains a high proportion of zircon. This process is in growing use in building and construction.

3 THE SUPPLY OF STRATEGIC MATERIALS

The dependence of the United States and of other industrial economies on a few sources for certain strategic materials was discussed in the first chapter. It is the intention of this chapter to provide, in the tables, details of existing production of the individual strategic materials and, in the text, information about the major deposits and potential sources of supply in order to provide a basis for the analysis later in the book of the potential for shortfalls or disruptions to supply for the various materials.

In identifying reserves and potential sources of supply, the lack of consistent international distinctions between resources, and the categories of proven, probable and inferred reserves presents a major barrier to making comparisons. The subjective nature and varying reliability of reserve estimates has led the Committee on Natural Resources of the United Nations' Economic and Social Council to recommend an international classification system for mineral resources, but this has yet to be adopted in practice by miners. In the absence of generally accepted definitions, reference in this chapter is generally made to reserves only within the context of the discussion of the economic life of the existing deposits of the country concerned. The reader should treat all references to reserves with caution.

Antimony

Table 3.1: Antimony World Mine Production (tonnes)

	1974	1975	1976	1977	1978	1979	1980 (est.)
Bolivia	14,912	16,089	17,015	15,156	12,672	13,020	15,465
South Africa	15,162	15,737	11,766	12,599	10,478	10,980	13,073
China	12,000	11,000	11,000	12,000	12,000	10,000	9,500
USSR	7,500	7,500	7,700	7,700	7,900	7,500	7,500
Canada	2,500	2,600	3,400	3,700	3,000	2,990	2,850
Thailand	4,236	3,133	3,670	2,454	2,873	2,900	na
Yugoslavia	2,208	2,183	2,021	2,500	2,760	2,810	na
Mexico	2,407	3,137	2,546	2,698	2,457	2,450	2,440
Turkey	2,295	1,550	1,784	2,032	2,440	2,450	na
Australia	1,406	2,205	1,892	2,089	2,100	2,090	
Morocco	1,850	1,052	1,426	1,285	2,110	2,090	na

There are four major producers – Bolivia, South Africa, China and the USSR – who account for approximately 65 per cent of production. There are six middle-rank producers (production between 1,000 and 3,000 tonnes), Canada, Australia, Mexico, Thailand, Turkey and Yugoslavia; and 6 minor producers (production between 500 and 1,000 tonnes) Austria, Guatemala, Italy, Peru, Spain and the USA. The US Bureau of Mines and other sources provide no details of antimony production in Guatemala, Peru or Spain.

In late 1980 the Bolivian antimony producers committee announced that it was to try to establish an international antimony council to assist in the commercialisation of the metal and to influence world supply.

Australia

A small-scale antimony mine and concentration plant is operated in the Hillgrove gold-antimony field east of Armidale, in New South Wales.

Austria

Production occurs as a by-product of lead-zinc production at the Bleiberg mine in Carinthia.

Bolivia

Presently the world's largest producer, Bolivia derives most of its production from the antimony smelter of Emresa Nacional de Fundiciones (ENAF) at Vinto which has the capacity to produce 5,000 tonnes of antimony metal a year. ENAF has been considering for several years a proposal to build a second 5,000 tonne a year smelter near Potosi but the market situation does not yet justify this new facility.

Canada

Consolidated Durham Mines and Resources Ltd operates Canada's only antimony mine at its Lake George property near Fredericton, New Brunswick, where proven reserves at the end of 1979 were 108,700 tonnes averaging 3.59 per cent antimony. The company recently discovered further ore near its mine and has now proved an additional 803,110 tonnes averaging 3.10 per cent antimony. There is also antimony produced as a by-product of lead-smelting operations primarily by Cominco Ltd, at its lead smelter and refinery at Trail, British Columbia. Cominco is able to produce antimonial lead with an antimony content of up to 23 per cent. Secondary smelters at Brunswick Mining and Smelting Corporation Ltd's lead plant at Belledune,

New Brunswick recover antimonial lead from scrap metal.

Antimony output of 1,700 tonnes per year is available from the Placer Development-controlled Equity Mining Corporation's Sam Goosly silver-copper property near Houston, British Columbia, which entered production in October 1980.

China

The largest and highest grade world reserves of antimony are located in the south-western Hunan Province, where the Hsikwangshan mine is the most important source, with reported reserves of 1.2 million tonnes of antimony ore. Second-ranked of China's antimony producing provinces but a long way below Hunan, is Kwangtung Province.

The Chinese are the largest suppliers of antimony to the European free market and at the end of 1979 established a stock of antimony metal in Rotterdam.

Italy

Tuscany is the source of Italian antimony production.

Malaysia

In May 1980 it was announced that a new antimony-oxide bearing mineral called sarabarite had been discovered in the antimony-gold deposits of the Bau Mines in the east Malaysian state of Sarawak.

Mexico

Considerable reserves of antimony have been identified in Mexico, mainly stibnite with some oxide minerals occurring in veins of limestone. The main deposits are in San Luis Potosi, Oaxaca and Queretaro.

Morocco

A producer with declining output down to only 550 tonnes in 1981, Morocco has minor antimony deposits at Masseraman, Tarilat, Mejma and Satihine.

South Africa

The country's only important antimony deposit is the world's largest antimony mine, Consolidated Murchison Ltd's mine near Gravelotte in the Letaba district of the northern Transvaal. In late 1980 the company announced that it had cut its milling rate from 45,000 tonnes per month to 30,000 tonnes per month due to declining demand.

Thailand

Production comes from several small mines scattered throughout the country. Operation of the mines has been intermittent.

Turkey

The Turhal mine in Anatolia is the largest producer and there are reserves in the Balikesis-Kutahya and Aydin regions

USA

Antimony is found in Idaho, Montana, Nevada andAlaska but production is concentrated almost entirely in the first two states. In Idaho it is recovered as a by-product of silver ores and in Montana from stibnite or antimony ore.

USSR

The main production of antimony in the USSR is from the Kadamzhay complex in the Kirgiz SSR. Output from this complex is scheduled to be increased by 50 per cent in the 1980-5 period. Construction of the new Aznob mine and mill unit in the Dzhidzhikrutskiy complex in Tadzhikistan, originally scheduled for completion in 1975, is expected to be completed in the mid-1980s.

Detailed exploration is proceeding on the Novae antimony-mercury mine in Kirgizia. There is increasing production of antimony from the UsT'– Kamenogosku lead-zinc complex and there are antimony deposits in Kazakhstan, Sarylakhand Tazhdolinsk.

Yugoslavia

The new Winogradi antimony mine in Loznia, Serbia was expected to begin operations in late 1980, with an eventual capacity of 1,900 tonnes of antimony concentrates a year. This will add to the country's antimony production of about 2,090 tonnes a year. The Rajiceva Gora mine and mill on Kopanonik mountain, developed in 1981, have an output of 120,000 tons of ore averaging 2 to 3 per cent antimony.

Beryllium

The USSR is the major producer of beryl and the USA is the only important producer of bertrandite.

Table 3.2: Beryl Production[a] (tonnes)

	1976	1977	1978[b]
USSR[c]	1,650	1,700	1,750
Brazil[c]	450	500[d]	400
Argentina	112	103	75
Zimbabwe	60	60	40
Rwanda	46[d]	55	28
Uganda[c]	55	45	25
Madagascar	17	15[c]	11
South Africa	3	3	4
Nepal[e]	1[c]	1	f
Mozambique	f	na	na
USA	w	w	w

Notes: a. In addition to the countries listed, Bolivia and the Territory of South-West Africa (Namibia) may also have produced beryl, but available information is inadequate to arrive at reliable estimates of output levels.
b. Preliminary.
c. Estimate.
d. Revised.
e. Fiscal year ending in July of year stated.
f. Less than ½ unit.
na Not available.
w Withheld to avoid disclosing individual company proprietary data.

Africa

Malagasy has beryllium from pegmatite deposits; *Mozambique* has beryl deposits at Haunt Molone, Gurne, Milange, Changora and Zambue; *Rwanda* has beryl deposits in the southern Congo-Nile area; and beryllium is produced in the Kamituga, Kirn and Orientale Provinces in *Zaire*.

Uganda has deposits of approximately 80,000 tonnes in Ankole and Kigesi. *Zimbabwe*'s production comes mainly from the Urungwe district and other production comes from the Fort Victoria, Gutu and Mtoko districts.

Argentina

A formerly important but now declining source of beryl ore, Argentina's 1978 production was 75 short tons of contained metal.

Brazil

Beryl ore is mined in Minas Gerais, Bahia, Rio Grande do Norte, Paraiba, Ceará and Alagoas, with most production coming from the Jequitinhonha and Rio Doce valleys in north-east Minas Gerais. Production is mostly small-scale and the beryl is exported after beneficiation.

India

In India there is a considerable amount of beryl distributed sporadically in association with mica in pegmatite veins. Large quantities of beryl are found in the mica belt in the Hazaribagh and Monghyr districts of Bihar, and at Idlapati in the mica mining area of Madras. There is still some beryl produced from the former major producing state Rajasthan at Ajmer, Jaipur and Udaipur.

The advantage of Indian beryl is its high content of BeO – 10 to 14 per cent.

Mexico

There are some small bertrandite deposits (not yet mined) in northern Coahuila, Mexico.

USA

The USA is the only commercial producer of bertrandite from Brush Wellman Inc.'s Spor Mountain mine in Millard County, Utah. US production figures are withheld by the Bureau of Mines but have been estimated at 7,000 tonnes in 1980.

Beryl occurs in the coarse-zoned pegmatites of New England, South Dakota and Colorado but domestic production is negligible.

USSR

The USSR is a major producer and consumer of beryl which is found in most of the pegmatites in the USSR. Beryllium-bearing pegmatites, skarns, alkaline (feldspar) metasomatites, beryl-fluorite-mica metasomatites, beryl-molybdenite-cassiterite-wolframite deposits, and also fluorite-bertrandite-phenacite and bertrandite-bearing volcanic and subvolcanic rocks are among the USSR's beryllium deposits. The best-known deposits are in Kola Peninsula, Kazakhstan, the Urals, Altay, Transbaykal, the Soviet Far East and the Western Ukraine. It is proposed to recover beryllium from the Dzhidmsk tungsten and molybdenum ores in Buryat ASSR, one of the sources of planned expansion of production above the (estimated) 1979 level of 1,800 tonnes of beryl.

Cadmium

Table 3.3: Cadmium Refinery Production (tonnes)

	1979	1980	Estimated Reserve Base
Japan	2,590	2,240	20,000
Belgium	1,420	1,510	–
USA	1,715	1,480	110,000
Canada	1,480	1,200	120,000
Mexico	990	900	20,000
Australia	800	960	81,500
Other Market Economies (mainly France; West Germany; Italy)	5,119	4,900	240,000
USSR (mainly), Poland and other Eastern bloc	4,166	4,430	75,000
Total	18,280	17,620	666,500

Australia

Cadmium metal is recovered in Australia as a by-product of lead and zinc mining at MIM's Mount Isa in Queensland, at Broken Hill in NSW and at Roseberg in Tasmania. Electrolytic Zinc Company (EZ) of Australasia Ltd is the major zinc and cadmium producer from its refinery at Risdon in Tasmania. There it treats concentrates from Broken Hill and Mount Isa that assay up to 0.2 per cent cadmium and Roseberg zinc concentrate which averages 0.14 per cent cadmium.

Canada

Metallic cadmium is recovered as a by-product mainly from the electrolytic plants of Cominco Ltd at Trail, BC and Texasgulf Metals at Timmins, Ontario. Minor producers include the Hudson Bay Mining and Smelting Co. Ltd at Flin Flon, Manitoba and Canadian Electrolytic Zinc Ltd at Valley field, Quebec.

East Germany

Cadmium is recovered mainly as a by-product of the smelting of zinc and other nonferrous metals at Eisleben and at Weida, Thuringia. Production is very small in relation to the country's consumption, however, and East Germany is a substantial net importer.

USSR

Cadmium is produced as a by-product at a number of lead and zinc smelters and at some copper complexes. The Leninogorsk polymetallic complex in Kazakhstan, which produced the country's first cadmium in 1935, is still the largest producer and has the largest reserves. Other main producers are the Balkhash polymetallic complex also in Kazakhstan, the Almalyk zinc plant in Uzbekistan and the newly developed Dzhezkazgan complex in Kazakhstan.

West Germany

Cadmium is derived as a by-product of zinc smelting from the lead-zinc mines of Goslar, Bad Grund and Lennestadt.

Chromite

South Africa and the USSR dominate the world supply position.

Table 3.4: World Chromite Production ('000 tonnes)

	1978	1979	1980	1981
Communist bloc				
Albania	989	1,016	1,080	1,143
USSR	3,175	3,175	3,357	3,266
South Africa	3,144	3,297	3,415	2,867
Finland	719	656	566	631
Zimbabwe	478	542	554	526
Philippines	540	556	496	445
Brazil	269	340	287	408
Turkey	376	454	399	399
India	266	309	319	336
Madagascar	138	128	180	159
Greece	37	44	43	43
Iran	198	136	82	30
Other (Cyprus; New Caledonia; Sudan)	109	115	103	108

Albania

Chromite is produced in the Tropoje-Kukes area, the Bates-Martenesh area, the Latajzone and the Korce zone. The largest mine is the Todo Manco mine at Martenesh. Both metallurgical and refractory grades are produced. Albania was the third largest producer in 1978.

Brazil

Metallurgical grade production comes from open-cast mines near Campo Formoso, central eastern Bahia and refractory material is produced from a small deposit also in Bahia State.

Cuba

The main production is from mines in the Moa-Baracoa area, which is thought to total about 30,000 tonnes per annum.

Cyprus

Mostly refractory grade but some metallurgical grade ore is produced by the Hellenic Mining Co. Ltd from a mine near Kakopetria in the Troodos Massif.

Finland

Outokumpu Oy's Kemi mine in northern Finland is an open-pit chrome ore mine producing 566,000 tonnes a year from the Viiapit. The total reserves are estimated at 20 to 30 million tonnes.

Greece

Refractory grade production occurs at Fimisco's operation at Eretria near the town of Velestino. Mining operations at Skoumska and near Mount Vourino, both in the Kozani region, are the sources of metallurgical grade production.

India

Some 266,000 tonnes were produced in 1978, almost entirely from the state of Orissa.

Iran

Until the revolution, Iran produced metallurgical and refractory grades from the Froumad deposit in the north and from a deposit in the Esfandegheh area on the Persian Gulf.

Madagascar (Malagasy)

Moramanga is a source of chrome and Kraomita Malagasy has a loan to develop a pilot plant for a 60,000 tonnes a year ferrochrome operation at Andriamena.

New Caledonia

Inco Metals Ltd is bringing back into production a deposit of chromite at Tiebaghi in the north of the island which is expected to yield about 85,000 tons of chromite concentrates annually when production begins.

The Philippines

In the Philippines, Consolidated Mines Ltd owns the Masinloc refractory chromite mine which has been operated by Benguet Corporation since 1934 under an agreement giving Benguet a 25 per cent share of net cash receipts. A new 25-year contract between CMI and Benguet was signed on 8 January 1981, after negotiations since 1975. The new agreement gives Benguet 70 per cent of net cash receipts and the obligation to meet the full cost of future fixed assets. CMI remains owner of the existing fixed assets and will get 30 per cent of the net cash receipts. Because of the prolonged negotiations no development plans had been organised, but now Benguet is speeding development of a major new underground mine in Parcel No. 1 of the Zambales Mineral (Chromite) Reservation which, when completed in 1985 at a cost of $US10 million, will extend the life of the Masinloc operation by some ten years.

South Africa

The leading world producer of chromite, South Africa has a major chromite resource in the Bushveld complex. The Bushveld chromite layers are categorised as Lower, Middle and Upper groups. Mining operations centre on the Lower group layers which have the highest Cr/Fe ratios. The Upper group of chromite layers, although containing Cr/Fe ratios of 1:4 or less and therefore not able to be mined for the chromite alone, does contain economic concentrations of platinum group metals that would allow chemical grade chromite ore to be produced as a by-product.

The main producers and their 1980 production levels are listed in Table 3.5.

All Bushveld chromite ore is chemical grade and was only sold as such until the introduction of the argon-oxygen decarburisation process which enabled high carbon ferrochromium to be used in stainless steel manufacture. Techniques were developed for the separation of chromite from platinum group metals and this has enabled the mining of the Upper group-2 chromite layer.

The Sudan

The government-owned Ingessana Hills mine is the main producer.

Table 3.5: South African Chromite Producers (1980 production in tonnes)

Company	Mine	Tonnes
General Mining Union Corporation	Groothoek Kroondal Montrose Zwartkop	2,000,000
Barlow Rand	Millsell Henry Gould Winterveld	2,000,000
Samancor	Ruighoek Mooinooi Grasvally	672,000
Lavino SA Pty Ltd	Lavino	360,000
Sherwood Chrome Mines	Ntuane	240,000
Mining Corporation Ltd	Dilokong	185,000
Consolidated Chrome Corporation	in Rustenburg area	180,000
Union Carbide Corporation	Jagdlust	150,000
Metallurg SA (Pty) Ltd	Waterkloof	120,000
Anglo American Corporation Ltd	Marico (Nietveriend)	110,000
Zeerust Chrome Mines Ltd	Nietveriend	100,000
Total		6,117,000

Source: Buchanan (1975).

Turkey

Mainly a chromite producer for the metallurgical industry. Etibank is the largest producer of chromite ores and Egemetal Madenclik AS is a producer itself and also acts as a clearing house for the many small producers. Chromite occurs in 40 of Turkey's 67 provinces and is produced by at least 39 mining companies and 20 one-man operations.

USSR

The major producer of very high-grade metallurgical ore is the Donskoy Combine in the Khrom-Tau area and the main source of chemical and refractory grade chromite is the Saranovskoye operation in the Urals.

Zimbabwe

There are important deposits of metallurgical grade chromite in the Archaean Craton and the Great Dyke. Reserves of the producing mines which are mainly in the north of the country, are between 200 and 300 million tons of ore. Production is mainly ferrochrome with a small amount of refractory chrome also produced. Union Carbide's subsidiary, Zimbabwe Mining and Smelting Company (Pvt) Ltd, is the main producer, operating mines at Selukwe, Mtoroshanga, Darwenale and Ngesi with a total production of 29,000 tons of chromite a month. Three new mines, the Magazine Hill, Iron Ton and Railway Block mines at Selukwe are being brought into production and other mines are being expanded. Rhodall is the other main producer and Rio Tinto has the dormant Francis, Great Dyke and Rutala chromite mines among its properties.

Cobalt

It is estimated that the world's proved and probable cobalt reserves are 3,670,000 tonnes of contained metal, and that potential reserves are 4,450,000 tonnes. Just over 22 per cent of the proved and probable reserves occur in Cuba, some 15 per cent in Indonesia and 12 per cent in both Zaire and in the Philippines. The remainder of the reserves are located primarily in New Caledonia, Zambia, Canada, the USSR and Australia.

The main miners of cobalt are Zaire, Zambia, Australia, Canada, the Philippines, Finland and Morocco. Belgium (which does not publish production figures) is estimated to be the largest producer of processed cobalt. Zaire, Zambia, the USSR, Japan and France are other important processors.

Table 3.6: Cobalt Production (tonnes of contained metal)

	1978	1979	1980
Zaire	13,300	13,000	14,000
Zambia	1,700	3,250	3,700
Japan	1,700	2,500	2,855
Canada	1,700	2,000	2,100
Finland	1,000	1,200	1,300
France	1,100	1,200	1,100
USA	300	200	500

Canada

Cobalt is mainly recovered as a by-product of nickel-copper mining by

Inco Ltd and by Falconbridge Nickel Mines Ltd. Cobalt is recovered from domestic and imported cobalt-bearing nickel feed by Sherritt Gordon Mines Ltd, at its refinery in Fort-Saskatchewan, Alberta.

China

At best the country appears to have a moderate supply of cobalt. The Jinchvan nickel suphide deposit in Gansu is said to have a cobalt reserve of 100,000 tonnes but not all of it may be recoverable because of its low grade. Cobalt also occurs in a complex metal deposit that contains copper, iron and precious metals in south-west Yunnan Province; in the large titaniferous magnetite deposit in Sichuan; and with copper in a deposit on Hainan Island.

Finland

Outokumpu Company's mills at Kokkala produce cobalt.

France

Production of nickel and cobalt from the Société Métallurgique le Nickel (SLN) electrolytic refinery near Le Havre uses nickel-cobalt matte from New Caledonia.

Japan

Cobalt is separated from copper-nickel ores at the Nippon Mining Co's Saganoseki smelter.

South Africa

In 1978 Rustenburg Platinum announced that it would be establishing a plant for the production of high purity cobalt sulphate from its platinum-bearing Merensky Reef. No more than 150 tons of cobalt metal a year is expected from this source.

Uganda

In the first quarter of 1981, Falconbridge Nickel Mines Ltd announced that it had signed an agreement with the new Ugandan government giving the company the exclusive right to extract cobalt from the mine tailings of the Kilembe Mine in Kesese. Reports place the value of the tailings at between US$800 million and US$900 million. The mine is to be reopened by Falconbridge who will also build a cobalt refinery (commissioned in 1983), a sulphuric acid plant and a fertiliser plant. The mine is in the Ruwenzori Mountains 380 km west of Kampala, an area believed to have considerable copper-cobalt potential and which Falconbridge is to explore extensively.

USA

Noranda Mines has the Black Bird cobalt deposit in Idaho which was thought capable of an annual production of 1,200 tonnes of cobalt. Sharply rising capital costs and the necessity to build a pilot plant to test the refining process developed for the project have postponed production in the meantime. Reserves are defined as four million short tons of ore grading 0.6 per cent cobalt and 1.2 per cent copper. As of 1983, market prices inhibit commercial development.

In June 1980 Ni-Cal Development Ltd of Vancouver announced a $2.1 million development of its cobalt, nickel and chromium prospect in Gasquet Mountain in Del Norte County, California.

Zaire

Générale des Carriéres et des Mines, more usually known as Gecamines, is the national mining company of Zaire. It carries on mining operations in five open-cast and three underground mines on an 18,000 square kilometre concession in southern Shaba. The company mines copper, with by-products of cobalt, zinc, cadmium, germanium, gold and silver. The sulphide and oxide concentrates produced from the copper-cobalt ore are leached in sulphuric acid and, after electrolytic extraction of the copper, part of the electrolyte is purified in the cobalt plant. The cobalt is precipitated in the form of a hydrate which is then leached in acid. The solution is then clarified and cobalt is extracted by electrolysis.

Zambia

Cobalt is mined with copper at Baluba in Luanshuya, at Chambishi and Chibuluma in Kalushi and at Nkana-Mindola in Kitwe. The latter is the main source of production.

Columbium

The pyrochlore mines at Araxa and Catalao in Brazil and at St Honoré, Quebec produce over 95 per cent of the world's primary production of columbium.

Table 3.7: Columbium Mine Production ('000 lb columbium content)

	1979	1980
Brazil	18,300	19,500
Canada	3,700	4,200
Nigeria	500	550
Zaire	20	20
Other Market Economies (Thailand; Australia; Malaysia)	500	200
Central Economies (USSR; China)	na	na

Note: na = not available.

Canada

The only columbium producer is Niobec Inc's St Honoré mine near Chicoutimi, Quebec which produces pyrochlore ore and columbium pentoxide in concentrate.The company's capacity of 2,500 tonnes of columbium pentoxide concentrate a year was increased by 30 per cent in 1981 due to expansion of both mine and mill. Niobec is owned equally by Soquem and Teck Corporation. Potential producers are the Oka deposit in Quebec which has 125 million lb of Cb_2O_5 in indicated ore reserves, the Moosonee, Ontario deposit which has reserves of 800 million lb and the Thor Lake deposit in the Northwest Territories which has indicated ore reserves of 800 million lb.

Brazil

Companhia Brasileira de Metalurgia e Mineracao (CBMM) is the world's largest columbium producer. The largest mines are Araxa which is currently expanding production to 55 million 1b a year and Catalao. A deposit at Tapira has 0.51 per cent Cb_2O_5 or indicated reserves of 140 million pounds of Cb_2O_5.

Kenya

At Mrime Hill indicated ore reserves of 1,400 million lb have been identified.

Nigeria

Production capacity is about two million lb a year.

Zaire

A potential producer is at Lueshe in Kiwi where indicated ore reserves total 450 million lb.

Germanium

Very few minerals contain 5 per cent or more germanium. Renierite, a copper-zinc sulphide ore yielding 6 per cent to 8 per cent germanium is found in Kipushi in *Zaire*. Production of germanium-rich copper-zinc ore from Gecamines' Kipushi mine appeared to have stopped in the 1970s and, although it resumed in 1980, no arrangement for processing had been made by early 1983. Reserves are at least 200 and possibly as much as 2,000 tonnes and this is the richest germanium deposit now known.

The zinc ore sphalerite is now the principal source of germanium although its heaviest concentration of germanium is only 1 per cent. The germanium is recovered as a by-product of zinc processing. The two major producers of refined germanium and germanium dioxide are the *Belgian* company, Metallurgie Hoboken-Overpelt, whose source of supply has shifted from Zaire to the germanium-rich residues of the Jersey Minere Zinc Co.'s zinc smelter in the *United States*; and the US company, Eagle Picher Industries, which has used stockpiled zinc residues form past zinc smelting operations and was reported in 1981 (*Metal Bulletin*, 10 April) to be using supplies from the *French* company Pennaroya.

The main European producer of refined germanium is Preussag in *West Germany* which uses germanium concentrates from both Pennaroya and the *Austrian* company, Bleiberger Bergwerks-Union. The US Bureau of Mines estimates germanium production in the *USSR* at 9 tonnes a year but Bartlett, Bear and McCall (1980) suggest that 40 tonnes a year may be being produced there. The difficulty in determining the level of production is that it is not possible to identify the mineral sources used in the USSR. Some germanium is also produced in *China*.

Since 1970, although there has been no commercial production in the *UK* using the GEC-Johnson Matthey process for extracting germanium from grades of flue dust production in coal gas plants, as the North Sea gas made coal-gas works obsolete, the potential supply from UK reserves of coal ash would be sufficient to ensure an oversupply of germanium on world markets.

Table 3.8: Germanium

	Plant Production	Kg of Metal
	1979	1980
United States	23,000	27,000
Zaire	na	na
Other Market Economies (France; Belgium; Austria)	77,000	79,000
Central Economies (USSR; China)	9,000	1,000

Note: na = not available.

Hafnium

Japan and the *USA* are the main producers. The planned expansion of Western Zirconium's zirconium plant at Little Mountain, near Ogden, Utah will allow the production of hafnium as a by-product. Nippon Mining's Toda zirconium smelting facilities uses zircon sand which contains some 2 to 5 per cent hafnium. Official production figures for hafnium are not published, both the 1981 *Mining Annual Review* states that according to the US Bureau of Mines, approximately 100 tonnes a year is used.

Indium

The US Bureau of Mines estimated 1981 world indium output at 1.4 million ozs and reserves at 50 million ozs. A minor by-product of zinc refining, indium is produced by the *USA* where Asarco and the Indium Corporation of America are the major producers. Most of the Indium Corporation's production is from the treatment of Bolivian indium-rich ores. *Japan*, the *USSR* and *Peru, Belgium* and *Canada* are other producers.

Lithium

Table 3.9: Lithium Production

	m. lb	
	1979	1980
USSR	1,300	1,300
Australia		
Namibia	260	200
Zimbabwe		
Brazil	60	60
USA	w	w

Note: w = withheld.

Bolivia

Lithium deposits were reported in 1979 in the salares or salt lake areas of the Altiplano.

Chile

A large proportion of the world's known reserves of lithium occurs in the potassium-rich brines of the Salar de Atacama in northern Chile. In 1980 the Foote Mineral Company formed a limited partnership with a Chilean government development company. The partnership, Sociedad de Litio Ltda (SCL), is spending $US26 million in capital costs for a project to produce lithium from the brine deposit beginning in 1984 at a rate of 12 million lb of lithium carbonate a year.

China

It is thought that the salt lakes on the Tibetan plateau may contain very large lithium accumulations.

Japan

The Honjo Chemical Co. is the largest producer of lithium chemicals.

Namibia (South-West Africa)

SWA Lithium Mines produces lithium at three of its mines near Karibab, but production figures are not released.

USA

The Foote Mineral Company (a Newmont Mining Corporation subsidiary) produces lithium carbonate from brines in Silver Peak, Nevada and lithium carbonate and other lithium products from an open-cast spodumene mine at Kings Mountain, North Carolina. A total of 27.7 million lb of lithium carbonate was produced from both sources in 1980.

The other major US producer, the Lithium Corporation of America (a subsidiary of Gulf Resources and Chemical Corporation), mines spodumene ore from a large open-cast mine near Bessemer City, North Carolina and produces lithium chemicals and lithium metal from its Bessemer City plant.

USSR

The main source of production is a spodumene deposit in the Ural Mountains.

Zimbabwe

Bikita Minerals (Pvt) Ltd is the world's major producer of the natural low iron (less than 0.1 per cent Fe_2O_3) lithium minerals used in specialist glass and ceramics.

Manganese

Table 3.10: Manganese Ore Production ('000 tonnes)

	1978	1979	1980
USSR	10,619	10,500	11,000
South Africa	4,759	5,713	5,000
Australia	1,422	1,836	1,800
Gabon	1,885	2,000	1,800
India	1,727	1,800	1,700
Brazil	1,100	1,875	1,600
China		1,650	1,000

Australia

One of the largest high-grade manganese mines in the world is at the Groote Eylandt operation on an island in the Gulf of Carpentaria in the Northern Territory. The Groote Eylandt Mining Co. Ltd, the mine operator, is a subsidiary of the Broken Hill Pty Ltd. The company has plans to expand its production to three million tonnes by 1985.

Brazil

The main source of production, the Serro do Navio mine in Amapa, is expected to be exhausted within 12 years but there are reserves thought to total five times Amapa's present reserves in other Brazilian deposits.

China

Although China mines manganese it is primarily low-grade. Deposits of higher-grade manganese ore have been reported in the south-west of Yunnan Province and in Daxin County, Guangxi.

Egypt

A feasibility study of potential manganese mining in the Sinai is proceeding.

Gabon

The country's major manganese producer is the COMILOG operation in which the shareholders are US Steel (44.1 per cent), the French BRGM (19.8 per cent), Cè de Mokta (17.1 per cent), the Gabon government (10 per cent) and the Soc. Aux du Manganese de Franceville (9 per cent). Estimates of reserves suggest there are approximately 200 million tonnes grading 48 per cent manganese dioxide. It is anticipated that manganese production will almost double the present level of production when the Trans-Gabon railway is completed in 1983-4.

Ghana

Production from the Ghana National Manganese Corporation's Nsuta open-cast mine is in the process of switching from metallurgical grade ore to carbonate reserves.

India

The main deposits are in the Sandur Basin, near Haspet in Karnataka which was discovered in 1980, in the Nagpur-Bhandara-Balaghat belt of Maharashtra and Madhya Pradesh and there is some manganese in most states. At the present rate of depletion, however, the government has become concerned that existing reserves may not last beyond 12 years and has been restricting exports, in particular those of high-grade manganese.

Mexico

Cia Minera Autlan SA de CV of Mexico is the country's largest producer of manganese ore from its mine at Tampico and it is developing the Naopa open-cast mine from which it is hoped to double the company's production by 1984.

South Africa

SA Manganese Amcov Ltd (Samanco) which operates the Wessels mine in the North West Cape is the most important producer. Anglo American Corporation's Middleplaats mine which began production in September 1979 is also an important producer. Both have substantial reserves and could raise their production above current levels if demand warranted.

Upper Volta

Manganese reserves of over 13 million tonnes containing 60 to 55 per cent manganese have been identified at Tambao in north-east Upper

Volta, but no plans for development have been announced.

USSR

With an estimated production of approximately 11 million tonnes, the USSR is the largest producer of manganese. The major source of production is the Nikopol in the Ukraine where there are 19 underground mines, ten open-cast mines and nine concentrators in operation. The open-cast mines are the main producers. The second source of production is the Chiatura manganese basin in Georgia, which has 24 mines and two more under construction. A minor amount of production also comes from the Dzezhdy and Atusuy mines in Kazakhstan.

Mercury

Table 3.11: Mercury Production (flasks)

	1980
USSR (est.)	60,000
Spain	50,000
USA	30,396
Algeria	30,000

Algeria

In 1981, 30,000 flasks were produced. Del Monego, an Italian company, operates a mercury extraction plant near Annaba.

China

Tongren in north-east Kweichow is the main producing area and deposits have been reported in Sunyang county, Shaanxi Province. Chinese production is approximately 35,000 flasks annually.

Italy

Formerly a major producer, Italy's Monte Amiata mercury mine ceased production in 1976 but resumed limited production in 1981 to supply domestic consumption. Very high production costs and low ore content limit any expansion of production.

Spain

Minas de Almaden is the major Spanish producer. In 1980, the company opened a new open-cast mine, El Entredicho, from which it expects to gain most of its mercury production in the future as its operations at Almaden become increasingly expensive at deeper levels. Annual production of around 50,000 flasks a year will be maintained.

Turkey

The Etibank State Mining Enterprise is the main producer, with an estimated 7,000 to 10,000 flasks a year.

USA

The open-cast McDermitt mine (a joint venture between Placer Amex Corp. and Minerals Exploration Co. of New Jersey) in Nevada is the source of most US production.

USSR

The world's largest producer of mercury, the USSR has its largest mercury complex at Khaydarkan in Kirgiz ASSR and its second largest in the Nikitov complex in the Ukraine.

Yugoslavia

In 1982, the Yugoslav government announced plans to reopen its Idrija mercury mine in late 1983. Discovery of a new near-surface orebody, estimated to contain 5,618 tonnes of mercury sufficient to sustain mining for 16 years led to plans to reopen. Production is expected to be about 8,700 flasks a year.

Other

Neither *Peru* nor *Mexico* are current producers. Mexico used to produce mercury from underground mines at Halikoy in Izmir and at Konya.

Molybdenum

Table 3.12: Molybdenum Production ('000 lb of metal)

	1979	1980
USA	143,967	147,000
Canada	24,633	30,000
Chile	29,892	30,000
Peru	3,440	4,000
Other Market Economies (Mexico; Niger)	1,400	2,000
Central Economies (China; USSR)	27,230	28,000

Canada

In Canada, the second largest molybdenum producing country, Placer Developments' Endako mine in British Columbia accounts for 50 per cent of production with its primary molybdenum production. Endako completed a major expansion programme in 1981. The other major primary molybdenum producer is Noranda Mines Ltd's Boss Mountain division near 100 Mile House, British Columbia. Molybdenum is produced as a copper by-product by Brenda Mines Ltd in Peachland, BC, by Bethlehem Copper Corporation's Iona Mine and by Lornex Mining Corporation's Lornex mine, both in Highland Valley, BC, by Gibraltar Mines Ltd at McCleese Lake, BC and by the Noranda-owned Gaspé Copper Mines Ltd's Needle and Copper Mountain mines at Gaspé in Quebec.

In 1981, production was expanded from a number of new mines. In British Columbia, Teck Corporation's Highmont copper and molybdenum mine and Amax's molybdenum mine in Kitsault began production. Highmont will produce 4.6 million lb of molybdenum a year and Kitsault expects to produce 9 million lb a year. Annual molybdenum output from Lornex Mining Corp's copper by-product operation is being expanded from 4 million lb to 6.5 million lb a year, while the Sullivan Mining Group subsidiary, Brunswick Tin Mines and its joint venture partner Billiton Exploration Canada, expected to begin production in late 1983 at an annual rate of some 600 tonnes of molybdenum disulphide from the Mount Pleasant tungsten-molybdenum property near Fredericton, New Brunswick.

Other Canadian molybdenum projects include Tintina Silver Mines' Red Mountain Prospect near Boswell River in the Yukon that Amoco Canada is working. Placer Development is evaluating Adanac Mining's molybdenum property near Atlin in British Columbia, and Rio Algom (70 per cent) and the Dickenson Mines Group (30 per cent) have equity in the Sieux Lookout, NW Ontario property of Pidgeon Molybdenum Mines on which drilling in 1980 indicated ten million tons of open-cast material grading 0.1 per cent molybdenum.

Chile

Corporacion Nacional del Cobre (Codelco), the state-owned mining company, recovers all of Chile's molybdenum as a by-product of copper mining from its four mines: Chinquicamata, El Tebuebtem, El Savador and Andina. The first two number among the world's largest copper porphyry deposits. Production has been increasing as the company improves the recovery rate from its by-product circuit.

China

China has molybdenum in its porphyry copper resources, in particular in a large copper deposit in Kiangsi Province. Its molybdenum production to date has been primarily from the Yangchiachangtzu mine near Chinsi, Liaoning Province which is reported to have reserves of more than 1.5 million tons. Another source of molybdenum is in the tungsten fields of Kiangsi Province. It is produced at the Malukou mines in Liaoning Province and the Sizhe mine in Xinjiang Uygur Province. It is thought that China may become a sizeable producer of molybdenum within the next ten years, with sufficient surplus to export.

Mexico

Mexico's first molybdenum mine began production in mid-1980. The mine is Cumobaki, on the southern end of the copper-molybdenum porphyry province in La Verde mining district in Sonora, 43 km southwest of the country's largest copper mine, La Caridad, which is adding a molybdenum recovery circuit to its mill to process the new mine's ore.

Niger

Molybdenum has been recovered as a by-product of uranium mining by Compagnie Minière d'Akanta since 1979.

Peru

Molybdenum is produced as a by-product from Southern Peru Copper Corporation's open-pit copper mines at Toquepala and Cuajone.

USA

The major US producers are the porphyry molybdenum mines of the Amax subsidiary, Climax Molybdenum Co., both located in the Colorado Mineral Belt near Denver, Colorado. The two mines are the Climax mine, the world's second largest molybdenum mine, and the Henderson mine which produces from the Urad-Henderson porphyry molybdenum deposit, the world's largest deposit. Amax also has the Mt Emmons property in Colorado and the Mt Tolman molybdenum copper deposit in Washington which are being developed.

Molycorp Inc., which has been producing from an open-cast operation at Questa, New Mexico, is developing an underground mine at the same place which began production in July 1983. Pennzoil's Duval Corporation produces molybdenum as a by-product from its copper-silver mines in Arizona and is the US's second largest producer.

The Quartz Hill deposit of US Borax and Chemical Corporation in the Alaskan Panhandle could increase US reserves of molybdenum by some 25 per cent but the deposit lies in a national monument area and clearance to develop may be hard to obtain. Other developing mines are the Thompson Creek deposit of Cyprus Mines in Idaho and the Richfield Co. subsidiary, Anaconda Co.'s Hall mine in Nevada. The latter came into production in 1981 at an annual molybdenum production of between 12 and 15 million lb, while Thompson Creek is expected to be ready for production in late 1983 or early 1984.

USSR

Molybdenum is produced in the USSR from tungsten-molybdenum and copper-molybdenum and molybdenite ore deposits located in eight areas. The most important producers are the Zangezur copper-molybdenum complex in Armenia, the Sorskiy molybdenum complex in Kraznoyarsk Kray (the largest producer in 1979), the recently-enlarged Mukulanskiy open-pit tungsten molybdenum mine, the Charukhdayransk and South Yashransk copper-molybdenum deposits in Tadzhistan and there is the Zhireken molybdenum complex under construction in Chita Oblast. The Erdenet copper-molybdenum mining and concentration complex in Mongolia, which has large reserves, was completed in 1979. The 1982 *Mining Annual Review* estimates reserves of molybdenum in ore in the USSR at about 200,000 tonnes. Of the other Eastern Bloc countries, Bulgaria and Romania produce molybdenum on a small scale.

Nickel

Table 3.13: Nickel Production (tons of metal)

	1979	1980
Canada	145,040	130,000
New Caledonia	89,550	80,000
Cuba	40,800	40,000
USA	15,065	16,000
Other Markets (Brazil; Colombia; Finland; Greece; Norway; South Africa; Zimbabwe)	318,061	290,000
Other Central Markets (USSR; Poland)	168,000	165,000

Australia

Western Mining Corporation has nickel mines at Kambalda-St Ives and Scotia-Carr Boyd Rocks (now closed) in the Kalgoorlie area of Western Australia. Seltrust and MIM have the Agnew nickel mine 400 km north of Kalgoorlie which is producing 10,000 tonnes of nickel a year. Freeport Minerals Co. and Metals Exploration NL own the Greenvale mine in Queensland which produces about 19,000 tonnes a year. There are high-grade massive sulphide ore-bodies near Mount Keith in Western Australia and other potentially mineable nickel deposits at Sally Malag, Kingston and Honeymoon Well, all in Western Australia. Although Australia has identified nickel reserves of some 7,900 million tonnes, only 1,500 tonnes are presently regarded as economic.

Brazil

The Niquelandia nickel mine and smelter project in Minas Gerais, financed by the International Finance Corp. of the World Bank Group, produces 5,000 tons of ferronickel a year. Companhia Niquel Tocantins (CNT) has an electrolytic nickel plant at Sao Miquel Paulista with an annual capacity of 10,000 tons a year.

Botswana

Copper-nickel matte is produced at the country's largest metalliferous mining operation, the Selebi-Pikure project.

Canada

Inco Ltd is the world's largest nickel producer supplying about 30 per cent of the world production. It operates ten mines, three concentrators, two smelters and a nickel refinery in the Sudbury district of Ontario; a mine and a concentrator at Shebandowan, north-western Ontario; two mines, one concentrator and a smelter and refinery at Thompson, Manitoba. The company has a further seven mines on standby. It has reserves of 395 million tonnes of ore containing 6.3 million tonnes of nickel and 3.9 million tonnes of copper.

Falconbridge Nickel has five mines, two concentrators and one smelter in the Sudbury area of Ontario, with ore reserves of 71.5 million tonnes of ore containing 1.1 million tonnes of nickel and 0.6 million tonnes of copper.

Key Lake Mining Corporation is developing two uranium-nickel ore-bodies in the Key Lake area of northern Saskatchewan and expects to begin production in 1983.

Colombia

A joint project by Econiquel, the state company (45 per cent), Hanna Mining (20 per cent) and Billiton (35 per cent) developed the first Colombia nickel mine in 1982. At a production level of 20,000 tones a year of ferronickel containing 35 to 40 per cent nickel, the mine is expected to have a life of 25 years.

Cuba

Cuba, which sells most of its output on long-term contracts with the USSR, has been rehabilitating and expanding its Nicaro and Moa Bay facilities and has built a third faclity at Punta Gorda near Moa Bay which has a capacity of 30,000 tonnes a year.

Dominican Republic

Falconbridge Dominicana, a Falconbridge subsidiary, has a ferronickel plant at Bonao which is now running at 90 per cent of capacity.

Guatemala

Inco Ltd owns 80 per cent of Exploraciones y Explotaciones Mineras Izabal SA (Exmikal) project which has an annual capacity of 12,700 tonnes of nickel contained in matte.

Indonesia

Inco owns 96 per cent of PT International Nickel Indonesia which has had difficulties bringing its Soroako nickel operation in South Sulawesi to full capacity production since its opening in 1977, due apparently to the silicic nature of the ore. The free world oversupply of nickel has caused two other projects to be deferred: the 50,000 tonne Korg Island project of PT Pacific Nickel Indonesia and the Japanese Development Co.'s Gebe Island mine.

New Caledonia

Societe Metallurgique le Nickel, SA (SLN) operates mines and a ferronickel smelter at Doniambo. It has made major expansion moves to raise its smelter capacity to 100,000 tonnes of nickel a year.

Philippines

Marinduque Mining and Industrial Corporation (MMIC) increased production by about 46 per cent in 1980 from its Surigao refinery.

South Africa

Rustenburg Platinum Mines and Impala Platinum produce nickel as a by-product from platinum mining. Matthey Rustenburg Refiners (Pty) Ltd built a new by-product nickel refinery to expand its capacity to 18,600 tonnes a year of nickel. The refinery started up in October 1981.

USA

Nickel is produced from laterite ore in Oregon, and as a by-product of copper production.

USSR

Second ranked world nickel producer, the USSR produced an estimated 155,000 tonnes in 1980. The main production centre is Norilsk in East Siberia where sulphide ores are mined. In the Urals oxide ores are produced in the Aktyubinsk area of the south and the Ufaley area of the central Urals. In the Kola Peninsula sulphide ores are mined in the Pechenga-Monchegorsk area. Facilities to increase nickel production are being completed at the Norilsk complex.

It is thought that known reserves in the USSR are about five million tonnes of contained nickel metal.

Zimbabwe

The country's six nickel mines work nickel sulphide ore-bodies. Total ore reserves are approximateley 60 million tons with nickel content ranging from 0.6 to 1.25 per cent. Rio Tinto operates the Perseveranco and Empress mines. The former was only reopened in 1979 and produces 13,000 tons a month, while the larger Empress mine produces 67,000 tons a month.

Anglo-American Corporation Zimbabwe Ltd manages the Bindura Nickel Corporation which has three nickel mines, the Madziwa, Trojan and Epoch. Additional nickel production is expected to be derived as a by-product from platinum mining on the Great Dyke. There is an occurrence of oxide nickel in the north of the Great Dyke and two nickel prospects in the greenstone belt that are potential sources of future nickel production.

Platinum Group Metals

The six platinum group metals occur together in nature in variable proportions and tend to be associated with large amounts of nickel and copper sulphides. Of the main producing countries only South Africa produces PGMs as primary co-products rather than relying on base-metal production. The South African deposits contain more than twice as much platinum as palladium; up to 65 per cent of the USSR's PGM output is palladium and about 25 per cent is platinum; and the Ontario, Canada deposits contain approximately equal amounts of platinum and palladium.

Table 3.14: Platinum Group Metals Production ('000 troy oz)

	1976	1977	1978	1979	1980	1981
Platinum						
South Africa	1,675	1,829	1,775	1,950	2,044	2,180
Canada	179	200	149	85	177	261
USSR (sales only)	600	693	263	375	334	295
Other mine production	31	33	31	31	310	30
Secondary production	130	100	150	154	310	340
Palladium						
South Africa	714	780	757	832	870	930
Canada	188	209	156	89	185	275
USSR (sales only)	1,608	1,075	1,278	1,412	1,214	1,285
Other mine production	37	43	46	43	48	48
Secondary production	270	268	332	454	349	330
Rhodium						
South Africa	81	86	86	96	100	
Canada	12.5	14	10	6	12	
USSR	84	87	92	96	102	
Iridium						
South Africa	42	44	37	38	40	
Canada	8	9	7	4	8	
USSR	56	58	61	64	68	
Ruthenium						
South Africa	216	230	229	256	268	
Canada	17	19	14	8	16	
USSR	56	58	61	64	68	
Osmium						
South Africa	27	29	29	32	33	
Canada	8	9	7	4	8	
USSR	28	29	31	32	34	

Source: US Bureau of Mines (1981): J. Aron & Co. (1982).

Australia

About 160 kg of palladium a year is recovered at Port Kembla as a by-product from nickel refining. Formerly, Western Mining had some by-product platinum from its Western Australian nickel deposits.

Canada

By comparison with South Africa and the USSR, Canada is a minor producer now, although until 1953 it was the leading producer. Entirely a by-product of nickel mining at Sudbury in Ontario, at Pickle Lake in Ontario and in the Lynn Lake area of Manitoba, at most only 75 grams of PGMs are produced per tonne of nickel. An estimated nine tonnes of PGMs were produced from these sources in 1980.

China

The shortage of electric power in the quantities necessary to extract PGMs in copper or nickel refining will limit the development of PGM production, but there are deposits of platinum and nickel south of Jinchuan in the Tsinghai Province, platinum and palladium deposits at Dali in the north-west of Yunnan and gold-platinum deposits in north-east Shandong Province and north Quingyan in the north-east near the Korean border.

Colombia

Platinum group metals come from gold-platinum placer deposits along rivers in the north-west. Companhia Mineros Colombianes SA recovers 70 to 80 per cent of production using dredges and the rest is produced by small one-man operations.

Philippines

The Acoje Mining Co. extracts a small quantity of PGMs from nickel concentrates.

Southern Africa

The southern African producers, Rustenburg Platinum Mines, Impala Platinum and Western Platinum Mines work the Merensky Reef which occurs in the border areas of South Africa and Bophuthatswana. Gold, silver, nickel, cobalt, copper and chrome also occur in this platinum-bearing reef which has been proved over a near continuous strike length of 140 kilometres. Typical composition of platinum group metals in the Merensky Reef is 60 per cent platinum; 25 per cent palladium;4 per cent rhodium; and 11 per cent ruthenium, iridium and osmium. The reef is mined at depths between 50 and 800 metres. As well as the Merensky Reef, the area contains two other horizons, the Upper Group chrome seams and the Platreef which represent long-term resources that will be developed when the Merensky Reef deposits become depleted. The Merensky Reef has vast reserves, however, and descends to depths presently unable to be mined so it may be well into the next century before the other two horizons are exploited.

USA

Platinum group metals are recovered from copper ores by an AMAX subsidiary in New Jersey, by Asarco Inc. in Texas and by Kennecott Copper in Utah.

USSR

Placer deposits in the Urals and at Aldan in eastern Siberia are the only primary sources of PGM production in the USSR and yield about 50,000 oz a year, but the major production source is the huge Noril'sk mining and metallurgical complex in north-west Siberia where the platinum group metals are produced as a by-product of nickel and copper. The composition of the metals is estimated to be 56 per cent palladium; 30 per cent platinum; 10 per cent rhodium; and 4 per cent ruthenium, iridium and osmium.

Though the Noril'sk complex accounts for about 90 per cent of the USSR's production, Monchegorsk in the Kola Peninsula and Peckenga on the Arctic coast are also sources of production.

Zimbabwe

Four nickel-copper-platinum complexes occur in the Great Dyke, with an average of 3 to 5 grams of platinum per tonne and associated palladium. *World Mining* in a report on mining in Zimbabwe in March 1981 referred to potential *in situ* ore reserves in two of the complexes, Hartley and Wedza, as close to 2,000 million tonnes. It is intended that the mines developed there will be primary platinum producers with by-product nickel, copper, palladium, gold and silver production. Rio Tinto already has a pilot operation at its Zinca platinum deposit near Hartley and a Union Carbide company, Mimosa Mining Company, is evaluating a platinum prospect near Shabanie.

Rhenium

Table 3.15: Rhenium Production (lb of metal)

	1979	1980
Chile	4,500	5,000
West Germany	4,500	4,500
Canada	4,000	4,000
USSR	2,000	3,000
Peru	400	400
USA	w	w
Other (Zaire; Zambia; UK; Sweden; Belgium)	600	600

Note: w = withheld.

Canada

The country's rhenium production comes from Utah International's Island Copper mine on Vancouver Island, British Columbia. The molydenite concentrate from which the rhenium is derived is processed in the USA and Europe.

China

In Tensing county in east-central China, Fluor Corp. is developing a major copper deposit which has recoverable quantities of rhenium. Operations are expected to commence in 1984.

Chile

Production comes mainly from the copper-molybdenum ore mined at the government-owned Andina mine. Chile is the world's major producer.

Hungary

Recoverable quantities of rhenium have been identified in the Recsk porphyry copper deposit in northern Hungary.

Mexico

The Caridad copper mine has an estimated 100,000 lb of rhenium content, although there is no evidence yet that it will be recovered.

USA

Rhenium is recovered as a by-product from molybdenum concentrate produced from porphyry ores mined in the south-west.

USSR

Owing to the few porphyry copper deposits in the country, rhenium is mostly recovered from flue dusts of copper, lead and zinc smelters and from molybdenite leaching. It is recovered also from molybdenite from copper-molybdenum deposits in the Balkash and Dzezkazgan complexes in Kazakhstan, the Kadzharan complex in Armenia and the hard-alloy plant in Uzbekistan.

West Germany

Approximately 4,500 lb a year of rhenium is recovered from Chilean molybdenum concentrates.

Yugoslavia

The country's newest copper mine at Veliki Krivelj is reported to be making the Bor copper complex one of the world's largest producers of rhenium metal.

Other

Peru, Zaire and *Zambia* also have rhenium resources now being recovered and, in the *UK*, rhenium-containing residues are recovered from molybdenite concentrates. *Sweden* produces rhenium, but from imported ore.

Selenium

Table 3.16: Selenium Refinery Production (kg)

	1977	1978	1979
Canada	410,326	392,777	511,700
Japan	456,386	453,600	453,600
United States	226,558	230,713	272,000
USSR	na	na	na
Mexico	50,000	80,000	81,000
Sweden	66,400	68,000	68,000
Belgium	60,000	60,000	59,000

Note: na = not available.

Australia

There is selenium in the gold-copper-bismuth-silver ore mined at the Warrego, Northern Territory mine of Peko Wallsend. One of Conzinc Riotinto Australia's (CRA) subsidiaries, Electrolytic Refining and Smelting Company of Australia, recovers selenium at its Port Kembla copper refinery and another of its subsidiaries, Sulphide Corporation Pty, Ltd has developed a process to recover selenium in the zinc refining process at its Cockle Creek refinery in New South Wales.

Canada

The largest selenium recovery plant is that of Canadian Copper Refiners Ltd at Montreal East in Quebec which refines copper from Noranda Mines, Gaspé Copper Mines and from the Hudson Bay Co.'s Flin Flon smelter in Manitoba. There is a selenium recovery plant operated by Inco Ltd at Copper Cliff, Ontario.

Japan

Selenium is recovered as a by-product of integrated copper refineries.

USA

Selenium is recovered at three major copper refineries: Amax Cooper Inc. at Carteret, New Jersey; Asarco Inc. at Amarillo Texas; and Kennecott Corp. at Magna, Utah.

USSR

The copper-molybdenum ores of Armenia have a selenium content of 3.6 to 10.5 g per tonne.

Tantalum

Table 3.17: Tantalum Mine Production and Reserve Base ('000 lb of tantalum concentrate)

	1979	1980	Reserve Base
Canada	285	340	2,000
Brazil	200	230	7,000
Australia	120	150	5,000
Nigeria	71	80	16,000
Mozambique	67	70	na
Thailad	35	40	10,000
Zaire	15	15	82,000
Malaysia	10	15	8,000

Note: na = not available.

Australia

Western Australia is one of the world's leading tantalite producers, with most production as a by-product of tin mining. Greenbushes, Shaw River and Wodgina are the most important centres of production. Greenbushes Tin NL, already a major producer though with decreasing reserves, received a new lease of life in 1980 with its discovery of a new tantalite deposit that may equal one-seventh of the world's reserves. The deposit contains 21.8 millon tonnes containing 0.11 per cent tin, 0.04 per cent tantalite and 0.03 per cent colombium. Elsewhere in Western Australia there are tantalite prospects in the Gascoigne region, at Kirup in the south-east, near Marhle Bar, near Norseman, at Mount Magnet and at Wodgina.

Another area that has tantalite prospects is Nicron Resources Ltd's leases 40 km south of Bynoe Harbour in the Northern Territory.

Brazil

Companhia Brazileira de Metallurgia e Mineracao produces tantalum concentrates from pyrochlore deposits at Araxa.

Canada

The Tantalum Mining Corporation of Canada Ltd's (Tanco) Bernic Lake, Manitoba mine is the only producer of tantalum ore in Canada. In 1980 about 159,000 kg of tantalite contained in concentrate was produced. Reserves at 31 December 1980 were estimated at 1,210,000 tons averaging 9.14 per cent tantalum pentoxide and there are 798,000 tons of stored tailings averaging 0.07 per cent tantalum pentoxide.

China

Tantalum is mined at Yi-chum in Jiangxi Province and a tantalum-columbium deposit in the Setai area of Xinjiang has been mentioned.

Malaysia

Stuverite, which contains 25 to 30 per cent combined tantalum and columbium, is produced as a by-product from tin-dredging and from old mine dumps where it was discarded previously. Tin slags also produce tantalum when the concentrate is smelted and are the more important sources of Malaysian tantalite – but these average only 2 to 3 per cent Ta_2O_5.

Mozambique

The country's tantalite resources include columbium-tantalite deposits at Haut Moloné, Mule-Vala and Dondo and tantalite deposits in the Zambesi Valley.

Nigeria

Columbite-tantalum minerals are produced as a tin by-product by Bisichi-Jantar and Vectis Mines Ltd and tin slag from the Makari smelter is a further source of tantalum. Production has been declining in recent years.

Thailand

Tin slags containing an average 11 to 14 per cent Ta_2O_5 are the main source of tantalum from Thailand. In August 1980 the Thailand government granted a locally-owned company, Thailand Tantalum Industry Corp. (TTIC), exclusive production rights to upgrade tantalum oxide from tin slags for a period of eight years. TTIC has built a smelter capable of producing 300 tonnes per year of tantalum and columbium oxides.

USSR

Large deposits of columbium and tantalum occur in the Lovozero massif in the Kola Peninsula. The USSR claims that these are the world's largest deposits. Two underground mines, the Karnasurt and Umbozero, are the present sources of production at Lovozero. There are other columbium-tantalum deposits in the Urals, the Ukraine, as well as in the Caucasus and Transbaykal.

Zaire

In Zaire the tin mines have been a major source of tantalum for over half a century. The principal source is the Manono deposit in the northern Shaba province, which is mined by Zairetain, a joint operation of the government and Geomines. Societé des Mines du Kivu (Sominki) operates the scattered tin mines in the Kivi-Maniema area of the northeast from which most of the remaining tantalum is obtained. Manono has been declining as a source in recent years as the more accessible parts of the deposit have been depleted leaving a reserve estimated to contain over 100,000 tonnes of tin in a hard rock pegmatite that requires different mining methods to extract. Sonimki's production has been increasing.

According to the Tantalum Producers International Study Center there is much controversy concerning the amount of Zaire's reserves. Estimates of 10.1 million lb of Ta_2O_5 have been made but there are also much higher figures suggested. In the absence of reliable information about the ratio of recoverable Ta_2O_5 to tin it is advisable to treat all estimates with caution.

Zimbabwe

Several companies are prospecting for tantalite in the north-east of the country and Corsyn Consolidated is prospecting east of Harare at Ancturus.

Tellurium

Tellurium is widely disseminated without forming an ore and accordingly there are no mining reserves as such but there are large resources in base metal sulphide deposits mined for other minerals. Most tellurium is recovered from copper, copper-nickel and lead sulphide ores (in which it represents between 0.1 and 5 parts per million) and as a by-product of copper or lead refining. Tellurium occurs in coal deposits as an estimated average of four times that of copper deposits, but the US Bureau of Mines regards the recovery of tellurium from coal deposits as unlikely in the foreseeable future. At present, most of the world's recoverable tellurium is in North America.

Table 3.18: Tellurium World Plant Production and Reserve Base ('000 lb of metal)

	1979	1980[a]	Reserve Base[b]
USA	w	w	20,000
Japan	170	170	–
Canada	104	100	7,000
Hong Kong	100	100	–
Fiji	50[a]	50	na
Peru	35[a]	35	7,000
India	1	3	na
Other (Australia; Belgium; West Germany; USSR)	na	na	75,000
World Total	480[c]	458[c]	109,000

Notes:

a. Estimated.

b. Estimated at 1980 prices.

c. According to the US Bureau of Mines, Australia, Belgium, West Germany and the USSR produce refined tellurium but do not report their output, while Chile, Zaire and Zambia, who are all major copper refining countries, may produce refined tellurium – but insufficient information is available to be certain.

w = withheld.

na = not available.

Canada

Copper and copper-nickel sulphide ores mined in the Sudbury, Noranda and Flin Flon districts are the sources of tellurium which is recovered at Copper Cliff, Ontario and Montreal East.

Fiji

Emporor Mines has developed a telluride leaching process which makes the economic extraction of tellurium from its gold-silver resources in Fiji possible. This began operation in September 1981.

Hong Kong

In 1979, Metal Refiners' (Asia) Ltd commenced production of catalyst grade tellurium dioxide and tellurium metal. The expected capacity of the plant – 130,000 lb a year – makes it one of the world's largest producers.

Japan

A limited amount of tellurium is recovered from copper ores mined in Hokkaido, but most of the tellurium production comes from processing soda-ash-slag-bearing residues supplied from all parts of the world.

Peru

The zinc-lead-copper ores mined in the Central Sierrian region are the main Latin American source of tellurium.

USA

Production from two refineries located in New Jersey and Texas recovers tellurium from mainly copper ores mined in Montana, Utah, Arizona and New Mexico.

Titanium

The commercially most important sources of titanium are rutile and ilmenite.

Table 3.19: Titanium Sponge Metal Production and Capacity

	Production		Capacity
	1980	1981	1981
Japan	21,257	28,000	30,000
UK	2,600	2,600	3,000
USA	w	w	30,700
Central Economies (USSR)	45,000	47,000	49,000

Note: w = withheld.

Australia

Although its dominance is expected to weaken in the 1980s with South Africa, Sri Lanka and Sierra Leone increasing in importance, Australia is the major rutile producer with 96 per cent of world output and 30 per cent of the Western world's ilmenite. Associated Minerals Consolidated Ltd is the largest rutile producer with mines in NSW, Queensland and Western Australia, current production of 150,000 tonnes of rutile, and 400,000 tonnes of ilmenite a year (as well as zircon) and reserves for a further 15 years of operations. The second largest producer is Allied Eneabba which produces 55,000 tonnes of rutile and 300,000 tonnes of ilmenite a year (and zircon) from its Western Australian beach sands mining operations.

Consolidated Rutile Ltd's North Stradbroke Island mineral sands operation in Queensland has a 15-year life at its annual production rate of over 100,000 tonnes of rutile and zircon. Other producers include Rutile and Zircon Mines (Newcastle) Ltd's New South Wales coast leases that yield 40,000 tonnes a year of rutile and zircon, Westralian Sand's west coast operations that produce 360,000 of ilmenite a year and Cable Sand's Bunbury, Western Australia operations that produce 130,000 tonnes of ilmenite and zircon a year.

There are potentially many more sources of Australian production but at least 30 per cent of these are unavailable for mining due to environmental restrictions.

China

There are ilmenite deposits along the shores of the South China Sea and near some of the large rivers. Ilmenite production is estimated to be about 90,000 tonnes a year, with rutile production of about 5,000 tonnes. The Japanese have assisted in the development of titanium processing plants. It was reported in August 1980 that construction of a titanium dioxide pigment plant in Szechwan with a 300,000 tonne a year capacity was under consideration. Titanium as well as iron and vanadium are produced from the Panzhihua iron making facility in Sichvan.

Ecuador

There is very little mining in Ecuador but deposits of titanium are known.

Sierra Leone

One of the largest dredges in the world, able to produce 16,000 tonnes of crude ore an hour, forms the basis of the Mogbwama rutile mining operation in the Gbangbama area of the Southern Province, which began operations in 1979. The estimated reserves are 53 million tonnes averaging 2 per cent rutile but a further 150 million tonnes averaging 1.8 per cent have been proved within an 8 km area.

Sri Lanka

The Pulmoddai alluvial/beach sand mines are the source of titanium and of zirconium.

South Africa

The vast titanium-rich beach sands at Richards Bay on the Indian Ocean coast of South Africa contain proven reserves of 700 million tonnes. Annual production includes 399,000 tonnes of 85 per cent titania slag and 130,000 tonnes of titaniferous magnetite.

USA

The US imports 90 per cent of its rutile requirements but it has a large potential source in western porphyry copper deposits from which it could be recovered, according to a study conducted by the US Bureau of Mines which was reported in 1981.

Tungsten

Table 3.19: Tungsten World Mine Production of Concentrates ('000 lb of contained tungsten)

	1976	1977	1978	1979
North and Central America				
Canada	3,790	3,994	5,045	5,726
Mexico	414	322	409	440
United States	5,830	6,008	6,896	6,643
South America				
Argentina	137	154	174	170
Bolivia	7,015	6,515	6,288	4,836
Brazil	2,120	2,672	2,557	3,000
Peru	1,303	1,160	1,283	1,100
Europe				
Austria	1,193	2,460	2,599	2,600
Czechoslovakia	175E	175E	175E	175E
France	1,396	1,440	1,340	1,300
Portugal	2,776	2,216	2,407	2,778
Spain	725	679	602	700
Sweden	428	439	1,279	880
USSR	17,600E	18,100E	18,700E	19,000E
United Kingdom	22E	172	143	50
Africa				
Burundi	4	4E	4E	4
Zimbabwe	130	130	130	130
Rwanda	952	1,252	849	850
Namibia	310E	330E	330E	360E
Uganda	240E	240E	240E	240E
Zaire	522	375	326	330
Asia				
Burma	608	613	1,038	1,550
People's Republic of China	19,800E	19,800E	22,000E	22,000E
India	51	62	46	50
Japan	1,786	1,693	1,678	1,700
North Korea	4,740E	4,740E	4,740E	4,740E
Republic of Korea	5,703	5,809	5,734	5,664
Malaysia	141	218	159	150
Thailand	4,519	4,859	7,026	4,030
Turkey	11E	13	20	140
Oceania				
Australia	4,384	5,198	5,910	6,907
Total	88,825	91,842	100,127	99,243

Note: E = estimate.

Table 3.20: Tungsten World Reserves, 1980 ('000 tonnes of tungsten)

	Proven and Probable	Possible Additional
China	952.6	1,814.4
Canada	245.0	317.5
USSR	215.0	261.3
North Korea	113.4	136.1
United States	108.9	326.6
Australia	55.0	75.0
Republic of Korea	45.4	79.8
Brazil	42.0	19.3
Bolivia	40.0	83.9
Other countries (Portugal; Rwanda; South Africa; UK; Thailand)	215.2	282.5

Australia

Tungsten ores have been produced for some time from tailings dumps of old gold mines at Westonia and Davyhurst in Western Australia. There is a tungstic oxide mining operation at Mount Carbine near Cairns in Queensland, a tin and tungsten mine (scheelite) near Sunnymount in north Queensland and wolframite is produced at Torrington in the New England district of NSW, but the major producer is King Island Scheelite's two mines at Grassby on King Island in Bass Strait near Tasmania. Wolframite is recovered as a by-product from Aberfoyle's tin operations in north-east Tasmania, Tasminex has a scheelite mine at Kara and there is a small wolframite deposit at Oakleigh Creek, both in Tasmania.

A major new source of production is the Mount Mulgine tungsten-molybdenum prospect at Mount Mulgine in Western Australia where estimated reserves are 61 million tonnes grading 0.145 per cent tungstic oxide. There is another potential mine in the Jervois Range in the Northern Territory where there are inferred reserves of between 100,000 and 200,000 tonnes of ore grading between 0.1 and 0.5 per cent of tungstic oxide.

Bolivia

International Mining Corp. is the main producer of tungsten, from mines at Chojilla, Enramada, Avicaya and the Estalsa dredge.

Canada

Canadian Tungsten Mining Corporation's tungsten mine in the Flat River Valley area of the Northwest Territories produced seven million lb of tungsten contained in scheelite concentrate in 1980. Amax (65 per cent owner of Canadian Tungsten) is bringing into production the Mactung property near the MacMillan Pass on the Yukon-North West Territories border where mineralisation is an estimated 63 million tons averaging 0.95 per cent tungsten trioxide. Commercial production was expected to begin at the Billiton-Sullivan Group's Mount Pleasant tungsten-molybdenum property in New Brunswick in late 1983. Up to 3.1 million lb a year is expected to be produced.

France

In 1979 Société Miniere D'Anglade's Salair scheelite mine produced 1.3 million lb of tungsten. The Bureau de Recherches Géologiques et Minieres has identified the Montredon tungsten deposit in the department of Tarn which includes in its reserves one million tonnes grading 0.70 per cent WO_3 and others in the south-west of France that could increase France's self-sufficiency in tungsten production.

Japan

The Chugai Mining Co's Tsumo mine which has 120,000 tonnes of ore with 0.4 per cent WO_3 is being developed primarily for its tungsten content.

Portugal

The main producer is Beralt Tin and Wolfram Portugal SARL's Pan Asquiera wolfram mine in the Beira Baixa Province. There is also a scheelite deposit in Tabuaco and a tin and wolfram mining operation at Argazelo.

Republic of Korea

The Korea Tungsten Mining Co. Ltd produces scheelite concentrates and synthetic scheelite concentrates at its Sangdong Mine operation in Kangwon Province. At the company's Taegu City metal processing plant APT, tungstic oxide and metal powder are produced. More tungsten ore-bodies have been located in the Uljin area.

Rwanda

Wolframite comes primarily from workings by tributors at Rutsiro and to a lesser extent at Gatumba and Musha, with other sources being

Somirwa (49 per cent Rwanda government, 51 per cent Geomines of Belgium), Gifurwe and Bugarama. 1979 production of 732 tonnes was well down from the peak production of 838 tonnes in 1977.

South Africa

There is a small sporadic tungsten production from the pegmatities of the north-western Cape and Northern Transvaal.

Thailand

Tungsten mining operations in Thailand are hampered by hordes of illegal fossickers. Operations include the Doi Mork scheelite field and the Doi Ngon wolframite field in the north and the Klao Soon wolframite field in the south.

Turkey

Etibank's Uludag tungsten deposit in the south-east of Bursa Province contains over 10 million tonnes of reserves averaging 0.5 per cent WO_3.

UK

A tungsten-tin deposit under development by Amax Exploration (UK) Ltd at Hemerdon, near Plymouth in Devon, has some 45 million tonnes of ore averaging 0.17 per cent tungstic oxide.

USA

The five US tungsten producing mines are in California, Colorado and Nevada, including Amax's Climax mine in Colorado and the Oxbow Tungsten Mine Inc.'s Mountain City mine in Nevada. Utah opened the Springer tungsten mine (the former Sutton mine) near Tungsten in Nevada in mid-1982, but closed operations shortly after it had determined production capabilities.

USSR

Although it is an importer of tungsten, there is sufficient domestic production to satisfy about two-thirds of domestic needs. The Tyrny-Auz tungsten and molybdenum complex in the North Caucasus is the main producer, and there are large deposits at Verkhne-Kayraktin and Akchatan (molybdenum/tungsten) in Kazakhstan and at Ingechke in Uzbekistan and at Jidola in Siberia. The country's deposits are mainly low-grade.

Zimbabwe

There are possibilities for tungsten mining in the country's many small scheelite and wolfram deposits, particularly in the Wankie area and in the south-east.

Vanadium

Table 3.21: Vanadium Production (millions of lb V_2O_5 equivalent)

	1979	1980	1981	1982
South Africa	48.6	50.0	46.3	43.1
USA	27.5	26.5	30.7	22.3
Finland	10.9	11.1	11.5	10.5
China	3.0	7.0	10.0	10.0
Japan	1.0	1.4	1.6	1.6
Norway	2.2	2.1	2.0	1.0
Australia	–	–	0.3	–

Australia

In the south-western province of Western Australia reserves of 31.06 million tonnes of indicated ore containing 0.56 per cent V_2O_5 have been calculated for the Coates prospect, 3.5 km east-north-east of Wundowie from which Agnew Clough began producing vanadium pentoxide in June 1980. The plant's full capacity of 1,620 tonnes a year is committed under existing agreements with Japanese and West German companies. The Western Mining Corporation's Yeelirrie uranium deposit 570 km east-north-east of Geraldton, Western Australia is expected to produce vanadium as a by-product. Alexander and Hattersley (1982) suggest that this could be 2.2 million lb of vanadium by 1984.

CSR has an oil shale deposit at Julia Creek, west of Townsville in Queensland which contains vanadium as a by-product. Ferrovanadium Corporation has a large titanium-vanadium-iron ore deposit at Barrambie in Western Australia. A 1980 investigation of the proposed development suggested that mining of 1.5 million tonnes a year could produce as end-products of the subsequent refining process, 219,000 tonnes of semi-steel, 188,000 tonnes of 70 per cent titanium dioxide (slag) and about 5,500 tonnes of vanadium pentoxide flake.

China

Reserves of 1,050 tonnes of 33 per cent Fe, 11.6 per cent TiO_2 and 0.3 per cent V_2O_5 are reported in the polymetallic titaniferous magnetite ore of Panzhihua, Sichuan.

Finland

Rautaruukki's vanadium-titanium-iron deposit at Mustavaara is Europe's largest source of vanadium.

Namibia

The Berg Aukas zinc, lead and vanadium mine has been the main source of vanadium.

Philippines

Filmag, the second largest iron sand processor in the Philippines, will produce a 15 per cent vanadium slag from processing Lingayen iron sand.

South Africa

The world's largest single vanadium producer is Highveld Steel and Uranium which produces vanadium-bearing slag as a co-product of its Witbank steelmaking operations and vanadium pentoxide from ore produced at its Mapochs mine in Transvaal's Middelburg district. The Union Carbide subsidiary, Ucar Minerals, has a mine concentrator and two refineries in the Transvaal, although production at one of them, the Bon Accord vanadium pentoxide plant, was suspended in August 1980. About 42 per cent of the world's vanadium production came from South Africa in 1979.

USA

Atlas Corporation, Cotter Corporation (a Commonwealth Edison Company of Chicago subsidiary) and Ranchers Exploration and Development Corporation recover vanadium oxide from co-product vanadium and uranium ores on the Colorado Plateau. The Kerr-McGee Corporation derives vanadium oxide from ferrophosphorus deposits at Soda Springs, Idaho. The Engelhard company, Somex Ltd, recovers vanadium oxide from ashes of Caribbean crude oils burned in utility boilers in the USA and Western Europe. The supply of vanadium recovered from Caribbean crude oil ashes is increasing and a further potential source of supply is from phosphorus.

USSR

Vanadium-rich slag is produced as a co-product with iron at the Kachkanar open-cast mines in the Urals, which are the main source of Soviet vanadium. The 1981 *Mining Annual Review* notes that the Nizhniy Tagil metallurgical complex is the only modern enterprise among the Soviet vanadium producers.

Zirconium (Zr)

Australia and the United States had been the only important producers until recently, but the Richards Bay resources in South Africa have now made that country also a major producer.

Table 3.22: Zirconium Production (tonnes)

	1979	1980	Reserve Base
Australia	493,000	500,000	16,000,000
South Africa	90,000	105,000	12,000,000
USA	w	w	8,000,000
India	11,000	12,000	3,000,000
Central Economy Countries (USSR)	large	large	6,000,000
Other Market Economies (Sri Lanka; Malaysia; Thailand)	11,000	13,000	5,000,000

Note: w = withheld.
Source: US Bureau of Mines (1981).

Australia

According to the Bureau of Mineral Resources, Australia has 14.4 million tonnes of economic reserves of zircon and 7.7 million tonnes of subeconomic zircon reserves. An estimated 45 per cent of the total reserves of mineral sands on Australia's east coast are frozen on environmental and associated grounds.

The main producers are Associated Minerals Consolidated Ltd which operates mines on the east and west coasts of Australia and produces 175,000 tonnes of zirçon a year; Allied Eneabba produces 100,000 tonnes of zircon from operations in Western Australia; Mineral Deposits Ltd produces from a number of NSW locations about 42,000 tonnes of zircon a year; and Consolidated Rutile produces around

50,000 tonnes a year from its North Stradbroke Island operation in Queensland.

Canada

Great Canadian Oil Sands Ltd and Syncrude Canada Ltd extract about 37,000 tonnes of zircon a year from tar sands. According to the Minerals and Energy Department of Canada, zircon is plentiful in the tar sands of Alberta, in mineral sands in Nova Scotia and in igneous rocks in Ontario and Quebec.

India

The country's 10,000 to 15,000 tonnes a year of zircon concentrate is produced as a by-product of the ilmenite production by Indian Rare Earths Ltd at Chavara.

Nigeria

Zircon is found in some rivers and streams and is also extracted as a by-product of the tin/columbite mining in Plateau State.

South Africa

The mineral sands operations of Richard Bay Minerals produced about 50,000 tonnes of zircon concentrates in 1979. Full production capacity of the plant is 115,000 tonnes a year. There are two other South African sources of zircon, both recovering baddeleyite (ZrO_2) concentrates at Phalaborwa in the eastern Transvaal. The Phosphate Development Corporation (FOSKOR) recovers baddeleyite concentrates from the treatment of apatite concentrates, while the Palabora Mining Co. Ltd produces by-product baddeleyite from copper mining.

Sri Lanka

Only about 1,300 tonnes of zircon was produced by the secondary separation plant of Mineral Sands Corporation in 1979 although the plant has a production capacity of 10,000 tonnes of zircon a year.

USA

Production statistics are withheld but the USA ranks with South Africa as the main non-Communist producer outside Australia. Production in 1979 was approximately 70,000 tonnes.

The main producers of zircon are Dupont's Florida operations at Starke and Boulogne and Titanium Enterprises Inc. which is producing zircon from stockpiled tailings at Green Cove Springs in Florida.

USSR

The Samotkan zircon alluvial deposits in Dneprovsk Oblast' in the Ukraine, are being exploited and technology has been developed to recover baddeleyite (ZrO_2) from the Kovdor magnetite iron ore on the Kola Peninsula.

Other

Malaysia and *Thailand* produce zircon as a by-product of tin mining.

4 STRETCHING SUPPLY – SUBSTITUTION AND RECYCLING

Economic theory predicts that under competitive conditions when the price of a product is raised, consumers will gradually transfer their demand to substitutes and the market share of the more expensive product will be reduced. The size of the shift following a unilateral price rise will depend on the comparability of available substitutes, on the price increase necessary to induce additional supplies of substitutes and on the time that must elapse before additional supplies of substitutes are available.

The strategic minerals discussed in this study vary greatly in their substitutability for particular uses. Because many of them are used in industries at the forefront of technological advance, the possibilities of a new material or process with the potential for substitution being developed may be higher than for other materials in uses with less technological change. It should not be thought that substitution could occur overnight, for even simple changes several years may elapse. The OECD provides a tabulation of typical development times for substitution systems, reproduced in Table 4.1.

Before drawing any general conclusions about substitution in the strategic mineral area it is appropriate to review each of the minerals in turn with respect to their possible substitutes. Scrap recycling is a means of deferring substitution problems. Its relative importance as a proportion of demand for each product is shown in Table 4.2. For the majority recycling is small or insignificant.

Another way of examining recycling is to extend a diagram provided by Schlabach (1980) to cover most of the metals listed in Table 4.2. This relates the extension of the life of each resource to its use growth and recycling fraction. Figure 4.1 plots the possible resource extension through recycling for nine of the ten minerals listed in Table 4.2 that have a positive amount of recycling. Antimony, with 66 per cent recycled, is the only one omitted. Antimony and germanium are in fact the only minerals listed in Table 4.2 with more that 30 per cent recycling.

Recycling occurs wherever it is economic to do so. In the cases where recycling is not important it is reasonable to conclude that it is still cheaper to mine new material.

Table 4.1: Typical Development Times for Substitution Systems

System	Development Time in Years
Non-interactive materials substitutions, assembly or component change.	1 – 3
Development of new material or chemical process.	3 – 4
Interactive materials substitution, electronic technology change, subsystem or smaller system development.	4 – 5
Systems of reasonable complexity.	7
Complex weapons systems.	10
Telephone exchange technology.	13
Time for scientific discoveries to find large-scale technical application.	15

Table 4.2: Recycling of Strategic Materials

	Scrap Recycling as % of Demand
Antimony	66
Beryllium	0
Cadmium	minimal
Chromium	9
Cobalt	8
Columbium (Niobium)	insignificant
Germanium	40
Hafnium	insignificant
Indium	small
Lithium	0
Manganese	insignificant
Mercury	12
Molybdenum	small
Nickel	20
Platinum Group Metals	16
Rhenium	small
Selenium	15
Tantalum	3
Tellurium	insignificant
Titanium	minimal
Tungsten	17
Vanadium	minimal
Zirconium	insignificant

Source: US Bureau of Mines (1981).

Figure 4.1: Resource Extension Through Recycling. Based on an OECD study and US Bureau of Mines mineral commodity profiles. The extension in time of the resource, t, in years equals: log (1/[1–R]) log (1 + [G/100]), where G is its use growth and R is its recycling fraction.

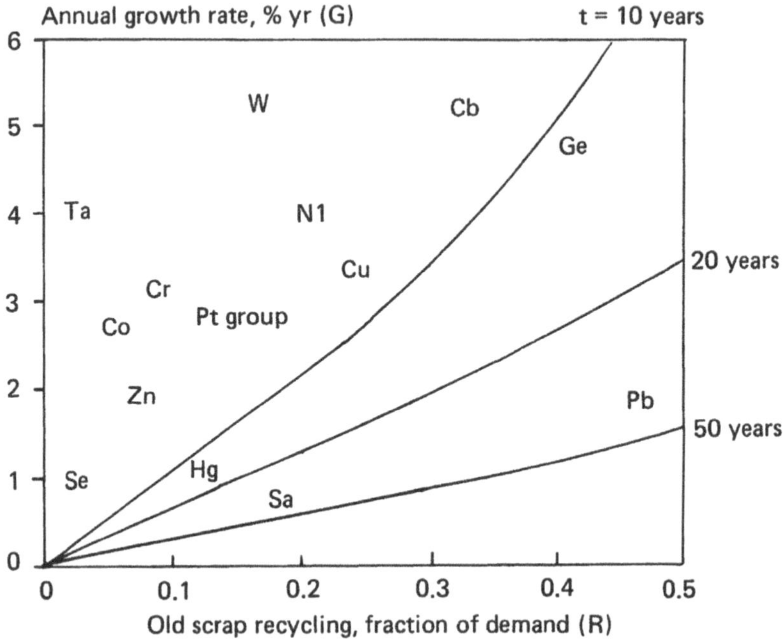

Recycling

Antimony

Antimony removed from batteries at the scrap stage is being converted to oxide form for use in flame proofing. This has reduced primary consumption of antimony oxide.

Beryllium

The technical problems of recovering beryllium from used equipment and the associated high cost mean that not much beryllium is recycled.

Cadmium

Because a majority of the uses of cadmium are dissipative, little scrap is produced. Only alloys and storage batteries have recoverable cadmium content.

Chromium

The US Bureau of Mines in two reports released in early 1981, which assessed the amount of domestic chromium that might be available in the US if foreign supplies were disrupted, showed that some 73,000 tons of chromium in scrap was lost each year in the US. Reasons for the loss were that the metal was left uncollected, used for lower quality materials or exported. An amount equal to 9 per cent of primary chromium consumption is recovered from stainless steel scrap.

Cobalt

Grindings and turnings produced in cobalt fabrication are the only real sources of recycled cobalt. The cobalt content of products is usually only a small proportion of the total product.

Columbium

Recycling is insignificant.

Germanium

Over half of the metal used in electronic and optical device manufacture is recycled. It is dispersed in, and therefore not recovered from, microelectronic devices. The new high purity optical devices are potentially a sizable source for recycling.

Hafnium

Recycling is insignificant.

Indium

With the dramatic increase in prices in 1978-9, secondary recovery of indium increased. Perhaps as much as 80 per cent has been recovered in some cases. The main source is alloy scrap material but the total quantity recycled is small.

Lithium

No recycling is recorded.

Manganese

At least some of the large amounts of manganese lost in the steelmaking process could be recovered from slags either by processing the slags into synthetic manganese ores (an uneconomic process at present prices) or by recycling the slag in the production process. The latter process is used to a limited extent in the United States.

Mercury

Almost all metal can be reclaimed from mercury-cell plants, electrical apparatus and control instruments on the scrapping of that equipment. Environmental control regulations require the recovery and re-use of mercury previously lost in effluents.

Molybdenum

It appears that only small amounts are reclaimed from spent catalysts or recycled as a very minor element of scrap alloy steels and iron.

Nickel

The US Bureau of Mines reports that in 1980 recovery of secondary nickel from old and prompt (spot delivery) industrial scrap accounted for 20 per cent of total nickel demand.

Platinum Group Metals

Refining from scrap in the US in 1980 produced 16 per cent of sales, and the quantity of toll-refined secondary production was three times larger. These metals are often recoverable because they resist corrosion.

Rhenium

The only rhenium recovered is in small amounts from molybdenum-rhenium and tungsten-rhenium scrap.

Selenium

An amount equal to about 15 per cent of world selenium production was recycled in 1980, mainly in the form of used electronic and photocopier components.

Tantalum

New scrap production of 400,000 lb and prompt industrial and obsolete scrap of 50,000 lb were recycled in 1980.

Tellurium

Secondary recovery of tellurium from catalytic applications may be possible but recycling is not significant at present.

Titanium

It is estimated that at present only about 1 per cent of titanium is recycled; first, because the metal is destroyed in many of its uses and, secondly, because in its more durable applications such as jet engines, not enough time has passed for any of this material to have reached the recycling stage. Titanium dioxide is not recycled.

Tungsten

About 17 per cent of apparent consumption in 1980 was represented by purchased scrap, and the US Bureau of Mines suggests that more could be recovered potentially from sludges and scrap.

Vanadium

Small quantities of spent catalysts, tool steel scrap and scrap iron and steel alloys do process a little recycled vanadium but only the first two are recycled for their vanadium content alone.

Zirconium

Recycling is insignificant.

Substitution

Beryllium, cobalt, hafnium, manganese, mercury, molybdenum, the platinum group metals and titanium (in some uses) do not have ready substitutes in their present uses, and apart from the platinum group metals their supply could barely be increased through recycling. Manganese, cobalt and molybdenum are present in deep-ocean nodules which may offer a commercial source for these three metals that could expand supplies.

Antimony

There appear to be substitutes for virtually all of antimony uses. Antimony chemicals used in paints and pigments may be replaced by compounds of titanium, zinc, chromium, tin and zirconium. Even in its major use of flame retardation, selected organic compounds and aluminium oxide are alternatives.

Beryllium

The use of beryllium has been concentrated in those areas for which there are no feasible substitutes, due to its relatively high price. The only alternatives to beryllium appear to be graphite, steel or titanium composites as substitutes for beryllium metal and phosphor bronze for beryllium-copper alloys, but these give much inferior performance.

Cadmium

Zinc is a substitute in cadmium's electroplating applications and other inorganic compounds may substitute for its use in paints and pigments but with a possible lowering of performance.

Chromium

Because chromium is highly effective and cost efficient in its uses, substitution for chromium by nickel, zinc or cadmium in corrosion protection, or by nickel, cobalt, molybdenum or vanadium in alloys is not likely at present. Allen Gray writing in the December 1981 *Metal Progress*, commented that

> The hardenability applications of chromium appear to be largely a matter of economics, and technology for substitution can be developed (p. 20).

Cobalt

No effective substitute is available for cobalt's metallurgical applications, and it could only be replaced in the chemical field by substitutes that perform at a much lower level, except in the case of pigments and paint where replacement would be easy. In recent years the high cost of cobalt has led to the substitution of nickel-base Iconel 718 for cobalt-based alloys in rocket-ramjet propulsion systems. Cobalt substitute alloys have appeared that reduce cobalt content from for example 63 per cent Co to 54 per cent Co-Ni and 58 per cent Co to 52.8 per cent Co-Ni. These alloys are used in engine valve seats and diesel engine parts. Amorphous metals are being investigated as possible substitutes for cobalt.

Columbium

Titanium and tantalum can be substituted for columbium in some stainless and HSLA steel grades; however, twice as much tantalum is required to obtain the same effect. Molybdenum, tungsten, tantalum and ceramics are possible substitutes in columbium's high-temperature applications.

Germanium

Silicon, which has the advantage of a much lower cost, is a substitute for a number of germanium's electronic applications, but germanium is more reliable in the high-frequency and high-power requirements. The possible substitutes for germanium metal in infra-red guidance systems

– zinc selanide and germanium glass – give reduced performance.

Hafnium

No substitute is now available for hafnium in nuclear reactor control rods and refractory metal alloys. In some refractory and ceramic uses zirconium oxide and metal can be substituted.

Indium

The cost advantage of indium is the reason for its use in preference to gallium for some alloys, but in its other uses, indium has available substitutes. In its use as a fusible alloy, bismuth is often a substitute for indium. Silicon is replacing germanium-indium in transistors and both carbide and hafnium are substitutes for indium in nuclear reactor control rods.

Lithium

Sodic and potassic fluxes are possible substitutes in glass and ceramics and aluminium soaps are substitutes in greases. Zinc, magnesium, calcium and mercury are alternative anode materials in primary batteries.

Manganese

There is no satisfactory substitute for manganese in the production of iron and steel which is its major use. Some substitution is possible in some other uses.

Mercury

There has been substitution on the basis of environmental concerns, but a typical result has been that of the Japanese chemical industry which moved to diaphragm cells at a high cost to consumers. Substitutes do exist for battery applications but none for wetted contact applications. Few satisfactory substitutes exist for most uses and these are usually more expensive.

Molybdenum

While it is true that potential substitutes exist for most uses of molybdenum, the substitutes would change or reduce performance to such an extent, that little replacement is foreseen. Because molybdenum was a cheap alloying agent for many years it was very widely used in industry, and even at much higher prices the fact that the United States is self-sufficient in molybdenum and not in some of the possible substitutes also restricts the potential for substitution.

As an additive to steels and alloys, molybdenum is only replaceable by other materials at a sacrifice in performance. Chromium manganese, tungsten, columbium, vanadium and nickel are possible substitutes and plastic and ceramics would be able to replace molybdenum-containing steels and alloys in some uses. In its refractory uses, molybdenum could be replaced by graphite but only with some resultant difficulties in operation. Molybdenum orange pigments could be replaced by chrome orange or cadmium red among others but no suitable substitutes are available to replace molybdenum in its use as a catalyst under high-pressure and high-temperature conditions.

Nickel

Although there are substitutes available for nickel in almost all its uses, they involve greater cost and lower performance. Solid-state electronic metals offer future possibilities of substituting for nickel.

Platinum Group Metals

Due to their relatively high cost, the platinum group metals are used almost entirely in applications where no satisfactory substitutes exist. It is usually easier to substitute within the PGM group than to use alternatives.

Rhenium

Substitutes for rhenium in its major use, platinum-rhenium catalysts, are continually being evaluated.

Selenium

Silicon, cadmium and germanium can replace selenium in its rectifier and semiconductor applications. In glass manufacture cerium oxide is a substitute, while in electronics, pigments and rubber-compounding tellurium may be used as an alternative. Tellurium, bismuth and lead may be substituted for selenium in the manufacture of freemachining steels.

Tantalum

Because it has much more capacitance per unit volume, tantalum is not readily substituted for in demanding uses, such as in capacitors for miniaturised electronic systems and for systems designed to operate at extreme temperatures. In less demanding areas such as consumer electronics, aluminium and ceramic capacitors are substitutes. Silicon, germanium and selenium are alternatives for tantalum's use in rectifiers, and for its use as an absorber of residual gases in electronic tubes, zirconium, titanium and mischmetal are substitutes.

In metal working machinery tungsten, titanium and columbium carbide can be substituted for tantalum carbide. The Adamas Carbide Corporation commented in the January 1981 issue of *Metal Progress* that

> A tremendous decrease in the use of tantalum carbide by demented carbide in manufacturing has taken place. This decrease is permanent and in place for the grades being coated by the chemical vapor deposition process.

Tantalum's corrosion resistance is its major advantage for its uses in the chemical equipment industry, but there is a substitution from glass, titanium, zirconium, columbium and platinum. In the aerospace industry the metal's use has seriously declined and it is now used only in some high-temperature areas.

Tellurium

In metallurgical applications selenium, bismuth and lead are substitutes, and selenium is also a substitute in rubber-compounding applications and in electronic applications.

Titanium

In its industrial uses there are substitutes for titanium in high-nickel steel and other superalloy metals, but they are not suitable for all of the present uses of titanium. At present prices no substitute threatens any use of titanium dioxide pigment, nor is there any substitute for titanium's use in the aircraft or space industries.

Tungsten

Tungsten lamp filaments and a number of tungsten carbide applications would be very difficult to replace at the present stage of technology. Titanium and tantalum carbides may be partial substitutes for some uses. Carbon fibre technology may be able to produce carbon filaments as a substitute for tungsten filaments in the future. Tungsten electrical contacts used in distributors for automobiles are being replaced with the introduction of electronic ignition in place of distributors.

Vanadium

In order to substitute other materials for vanadium in its steel uses, higher costs must be incurred. Columbium, molybdenum, manganese, titanium and tungsten are possible substitutes in those uses. Platinum is a possible substitute for vanadium compounds as catalysts in chemical processes.

Zirconium

In some foundry applications chromite and some aluminium silicate materials may be used as substitutes.

5 SUPPLY DISRUPTIONS OR RESTRICTIONS, CONCENTRATION AND THE POSSIBILITY OF CARTELS

In this chapter attention is drawn to certain aspects of the supply of strategic materials that have been the subject of concern in recent years: the possibility of supply disruptions or restrictions, and the concentration of production in a few hands which may raise the possibility of cartels.

The introductory chapter pointed out the dependence of the United States and other industrialised countries on a few sources for the supply of a number of strategic materials and Chapter 3 identified the main sources of supply for each of the materials. In the first part of this chapter each of the materials is considered in turn with regard to the possibilities of supply disruptions or restrictions, while in the second part the significance of concentration in the context of the possibility of cartels is discussed.

Possibilities of Supply Disruptions or Restrictions: Materials

Antimony

While the four major producers (Bolivia, South Africa, China and the USSR) do account for 65 per cent of production, there are numerous medium and small producers and supply disruption appears unlikely.

Beryllium

The USA and the USSR are the main sources of bertrandite and beryl respectively, but there are other possible sources. Exhaustion of US supplies would increase vulnerability.

Cadmium

The only potential threat to supplies of cadmium appears to be a serious decline in the demand for zinc, from which cadmium is derived as a by-product.

Chromite

The dominance of South Africa and the USSR cause some concern owing to the lack of substitutes for chromite in stainless steel uses in jet engines, the nuclear power industry and oil refining. The Klass (1980) study of the possibilities of disruptions in chromite supplies concludes that a supply crisis (and high prices) would push a number of users to turn to substitutes and that supplies may then be insufficient for its more critical end uses. The main danger that they see is that a disruption in southern Africa might encourage collusion among the USSR and Turkey.

Cobalt

There has already been a disruption to the cobalt market due to the invasion of Shaba Province in Zaire. This event pushed up the price of cobalt tenfold.

Columbium

More than 95 per cent of the Western world's supplies come from three companies mining pyrochlore deposits in Brazil and Canada. The few sources create vulnerability to almost any type of production restriction.

Germanium

The market is very small and in the past few years has seen considerable price increases as demand grew faster than supply. Potentially there are more sources of supply than are used currently. In the event of a disruption these could be accessed.

Hafnium

Japan and the USA are the main producers. Hafnium is a by-product of zirconium which is produced from mineral sands. Environmental restrictions limiting the mining of beach sands have been important in some producing countries but the main limitation to the supply of hafnium is the demand for zirconium.

Indium

Zinc refining is the source of indium and this is the main potential limitation to its supply.

Lithium

There are a number of producers and several potential new sources have been identified recently.

Manganese

Crowson (1977) noted that if the South African source of manganese was cut off for the UK, British steel production would have to be reduced by 53 per cent. Industry stocks in the United States are estimated to amount to about ten months of consumption. In addition to South Africa, which supplies about a third of the Western world's supplies, Australia, Gabon and Brazil are also significant producers. In the long run manganese nodules from the ocean floor offer an unlimited source of supply but prices would need to be much higher than in recent experience to bring this source into production.

Mercury

Declining mercury prices in the middle and late 1970s reduced the number of producers but more encouraging price trends are bringing back some producers. Spain and the USSR are the major producers but the USA is also a substantial producer.

Molybdenum

Sufficient new molybdenum mines have been developed in the last few years in the USA and Canada to create an oversupply situation. Nevertheless, short-term disruptions have occurred. For example, the *Wall Street Journal* commented on 20 June 1979

> Unexpected production cutbacks due to occurrences such as rock slide and storm damage at Molycorp's Questa Mine in New Mexico and the current strike at Placer Development Corporation's Endako mine in Canada also helped to exhaust molybdenum inventories, which are currently almost non-existent (p. 30).

Nickel

There are a large number of countries in which nickel is produced and Canada, Australia and the USA are significant producers. Strikes have been a threat to Canadian supplies on several occasions.

Platinum Group Metals

South Africa and the USSR are the dominant world producers of platinum and palladium, the major platinum group metals. While disruptions to their supplies on world markets would be serious, it has been common for users to hold large stocks which would take more than a year to use up if supply stopped.

Rhenium

Chile is the main producer; however, rhenium is recoverable from flue dusts of copper, lead and zinc smelters and from molybdenite concentrates and there appear to be sufficient potential sources to make any attempt to restrict production by present producers unlikely to succeed.

Selenium

Because production is dependent on refined copper output it comes from too many countries for production restriction to be organised by producers and, in any case, there is an increasing amount of secondary recovery. Serious reductions in copper production could lead to restricted supply.

Tantalum

Canada, Brazil and Australia are the main world producers but Zaire and Nigeria have the world's main reserves and Malaysia and Thailand also have more reserves than existing producers. The main producers do not seem to be in a position to establish a cartel in those circumstances.

Tellurium

The presence of tellurium in many base metal sulphide deposits offers potential to increase production if there was any shortfall from existing sources.

Titanium

The only possible threat to supply appears to be the threat that environmental restrictions pose to mining. For example, 45 per cent of the known mineral sands on the east coast of Australia are frozen by environmental legislation.

Tungsten

There are large reserves in China, Canada, the USSR, North Korea and the United States. Restriction of supply from the Communist countries would not produce a critical situation.

Vanadium

South Africa and the USSR are the main producers and have the largest reserves. Australia is expected to become an important producer during the 1980s. The dominance of the main producers and the few producing countries could pose a threat to future supply. Molybdenum, which is now in ample supply, may be a sufficiently close substitute to make the restriction of the supply of vanadium more an apparent than a real threat.

Zirconium

Australia has been the major supplier. Details of the attempted zircon cartel are discussed later in this chapter.

Estimating Political Risk

The preceding examination of the possibilities of supply disruption for the individual strategic materials reveals that only a few of them appear vulnerable to these disruptions, due to the heavy concentration of production in only one or two countries. The risks of supply disruption in particular countries are hard to assess because the burgeoning literature on these 'non-economic' or 'political risks' has not yet produced a satisfactory technique of assessment. Table 5.1 summarises a number of the better-known methods of assessing these risks. The qualitative nature of the basic information used in these assessments, the lack of a formal means of generating a consensus among the experts consulted for qualitative judgements and the lack of a coherent theory able to assign weights to the various factors incorporated in the estimates, all suggest that the utility of political risk studies may be fairly minimal.

Table 5.1: Non-Economic or Political Risk Analysis

	Information Used	Form of Output
Frost and Sullivan (1981)	Three or more experts provide opinions on each of 63 countries	Table of probabilities of occurrence of each
Hudson Institute (1981)	Time series of events and opinions	Political Tension Index
Rummel and Heenan (1978)	Time series of events (e.g. riots) and factors (GNP)	
Haendel, West and Meadow (1975)	Time series of events and factors in 65 less-developed countries	Political System Stability Index
Haner (1975)	160 individual experts, with the opinions of five to ten pooled for each of 45 countries	Index number ranking for each country now and in five years' time

Szuprowicz (1981) constructs a national vulnerability index, an industry vulnerability index and a corporate vulnerability index but comments

> A system of this type is only as good as the information it contains; therefore it is important that reliable and consistent sources of information are used to develop the risk factors for these applications (p. 28a).

Table 5.2 reproduces the political risk assessment made by West Germany in 1979 for those strategic materials with which the present study is concerned. Chromium and manganese were rated the highest on the index scale.

Table 5.2: West German Raw Materials Political Risk Factor Index (selected materials)

	Index
High Risk	500
Chromium	370
Manganese	300
Tungsten	290
Cobalt	280
Vanadium	280
Titanium	270
Platinum	270
Nickel	225
Molybdenum	225
Low Risk	100

Source: *The Economist* (1979).

Environmental Considerations and Regulations

In many Western economies there is an increasing tension between resource development and environmental and conservationist ideals. Many communities are opposed to the development of mines within or near their boundaries because of the alleged adverse environmental effects and this restricts the development of new mines. In the United States in 1968, 17 per cent of all Federal lands had been withdrawn from mining and exploration activities but between 1968 and 1975 more withdrawals of land were made and by 1975, 67 per cent of all Federal land had been withdrawn.

Requirements for pollution abatement and for rehabilitation expenditure add to the cost of mining operations and must raise the threshold level necessary for the development of a new deposit. The increased utilisation of lower grade ores over time threatens to escalate the existing problem of waste disposal and will increase the space taken for each new mining operation.

Associated with environmental concerns has been a growth of environmental regulation that has added a major element of costs to mining operations. Ridinger (1980) reports that his US mining company is subject to regulation by 54 Federal departments and agencies, 42 state boards and commissions and 35 local authorities, of which 68 require reports from the company, 29 tax the company and 87 provide services. The total cost of regulation to the company, Ridinger estimates, adds between 10 and 15 cents a pound to its copper prices. John Goth (1980) of Amax commented on the costs of regulation for the two Amax molybdenum mines in Colorado that

> we can directly attribute additional yearly expenses of $7.5 million to the enactment and enforcement of just one new federal law, the Mine Safety and Health Act of 1977 (p. 17).

and the new law had not resulted in a commensurate change in health and safety for the mines' employees.

Stockpiling

The purpose of stockpiling is to provide protection against possible disruptions of supply. The introduction of stockpiling of strategic materials by governments may lead to higher prices as the inventories are purchased but may lead to overproduction capacity after the purchases for inventory are completed. Private stockpiles accumulated by strategic material funds may have a similar effect if their planned inventories are of any real size.

Once stockpiles are in place there is the risk of government selling to be taken into account in the subsequent pricing and supply of the strategic materials. Salant and Henderson (1978) show that attempts to limit the price of an exhaustible resource by means of a buffer stock 'inevitably result in a speculative attack' (p. 645). While the specific application of the Salant and Henderson analysis is to the gold market, it can be easily demonstrated that similar results obtain for other exhaustible resources (see also Long (1975)).

Figure 5.1 summarises the Salant and Henderson conclusions of the effects of the anticipation of government sales when private holders are risk-neutral. Following the basic theory of exhaustible resources developed by Hotelling (1931) path AA in Figure 5.1 shows the price rising over time at the rate of interest; that is the price path that would exist if there was no possibility of government selling. If there is anticipation that the government will sell from its stockpile in the future then the price path BB would be appropriate. Path BB has a slope that is always greater than that of AA and its slope rises as time passes. This greater slope is accounted for by the fact that risk-neutral private holders will need the price to rise by more than the interest rate in order to justify their continuing to hold it in the face of a possible capital loss. Should the private holders be risk-averse rather than risk-neutral it would be necessary for the return to the private holders to incorporate a risk premium and that would be reflected in a steeper rise in the price path than is shown by path BB.

The third path in Figure 5.1, path CC, reflects the price that would emerge potentially each period in which the government auctioned its stock. Path CC rises at a rate which is always below the rate of interest.

Prior to an auction but in continued anticipation of sales that have not yet occurred the price would move along path BB, jumping on the announcement of an auction to path CC which reflects the fall in market value of the existing stock. Price will rise from CC along a line parallel to AA.

Unanticipated reports of planned auctions would trigger price declines even if no auction actually took place as holders sell fast when faced with an increased probability of capital loss. The price path followed after the price decline will be lower and steeper when there is a positive probability of a government auction compared to the position where there is no chance of a government auction.

It follows that the existence of a government stockpile may lead to reports of expected sales and in some cases actual sales and that these will render the price of the material concerned more volatile than if the stockpile did not exist. This volatility is likely to disrupt the plans of producers and consumers of the material. Price Pc in Figure 5.1, the price at which demand is choked off, will be reached faster along path BB than along AA and this threatens disruption of the market and increases moves to substitute other materials where at all possible. The

Figure 5.1: Stockpile Sales and Metal Prices

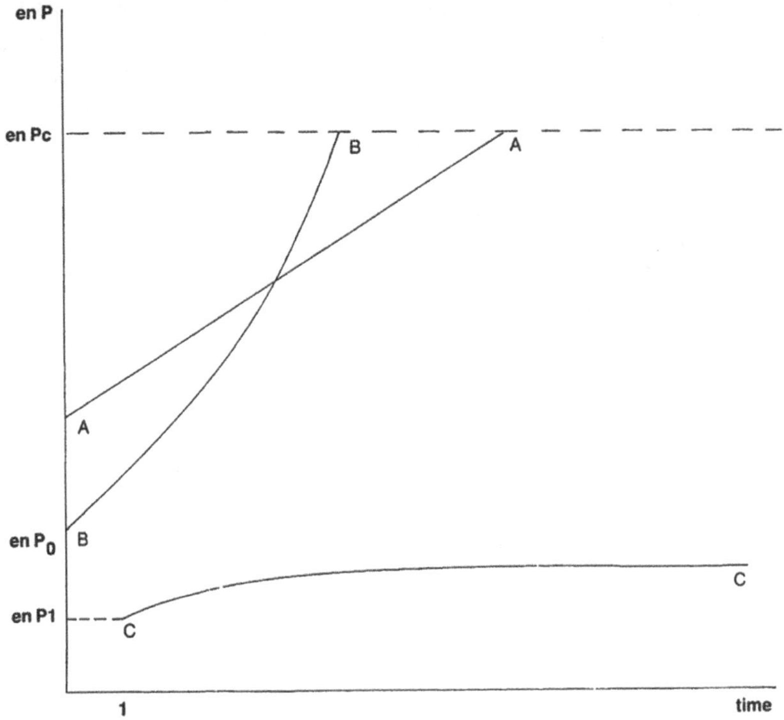

choking off of demand may have disastrous long-run consequences for the industry as could be seen, for example, in the response to the high price of silver in late 1979 and early 1980 which lead to widespread disruption in the user side of the market and, eventually, to prices being heavily depressed and production discouraged until at least mid-1982.

The Possibility of Cartels

A cartel is a collusive price-fixing arrangement made between producers not only excluding consumers, but also without consideration of the interest of consumers.

It should be emphasised initially that the risk of a cartel being established successfully in a majority of the strategic materials has been overstated. The presence of substitutes at prices close to the marginal cost and the availability of actual or potential production outside the control of the members of a prospective cartel are stumbling blocks that are very difficult to overcome. Further, there are other impediments to an organised restriction of production in the ability of consumers to stockpile, in the existence and possible expansion of secondary supply, and in the often dominant influences of demand rather than supply on the determination of price. The main usage of most of the strategic materials lies in durables, the working lives of which could conceivably be extended in response to the actions of a cartel. There is also the continuous stream of technological advances occurring in the industries in which the use of strategic materials is concentrated. The pressures to make such a technological advance would probably increase in the case of a strategic material that was the subject of an effective cartel.

In order to consider the possibilities of a cartel in various strategic materials it is instructive to consider in detail the attempts in mercury and in zircon.

The Mercury Cartel

Because production in the two major mercury producing countries, Spain and Italy, was dominated by a few companies, it was possible for the two major companies, Spain's Almaden and Italy's Monte Amiata, to operate a cartel during the period 1928 to 1949. The cartel fixed prices and divided up the world market, with Monte Amiata supplying the European market and Almaden, the North American market. This cartel disappeared in 1949 when the Italian company made large mercury sales to the United States, which had been in Almaden's exclusive territory. The cartel reappeared in 1958 and survived until 1962 when it was met by the EEC antitrust laws.

In 1972, when the market price for mercury had fallen from US$441 a flask in the late 1960s to US$170.95 in New York (and only US$153.30 in London), Almaden and Monte Amiata announced a minimum price of US$170.00 a flask and a new association of Mexico's many small producers agreed to defend a floor price of US$200 a flask.

In January 1973 Algeria (a new producer) and Yugoslavia joined the Italian, Spanish and Mexican producers in proposing a uniform floor price of US$300 an ounce which exceeded the then New York market price by US$15. While the higher than floor prices for the first quarter of 1973 must have encouraged the producers, by June the price had fallen to US$262.50. In July the producers met again and set a floor price of US$320 to be reached gradually over the following six months, and decided not to sell to dealers directly unless they had proof of an actual sale to a consumer. In order to prevent diversions of their production by agents, they intended to invoice mercury sales themselves and to ship the material directly.

In October the producers were joined by Peru, and decided on a new support price of $250 per flask to be raised to $280 in November and to $290–300 in December. In mid—May of 1974, Algeria, Italy, Mexico, Spain, Turkey and Yugoslavia, who between them accounted for some 90 per cent of world production, agreed to set a floor price of $350 per flask and to support this price by stockpiling the metal. By that time world production exceeded demand by ten per cent and in mid-July, after a brief rise in prices, both dealers and producers began to sell their stocks. Prices continued to fall and in mid-December a German soda-alkaline producer dumped about 2,000 flasks of mercury on the market, pushing the price down to $190 per flask.

With the depressed market continuing into 1975, Canada's Cominco closed its operations and many of Mexico's small producers closed down, but Spain, Italy and Yugoslavia with state-owned production continued production at their usual levels.

Producers met early in the year and again in mid-June but were unable to set a floor price that had any relevance in a declining market, even by the formation of the International Association of Mercury Producers (ASSIMER). During this year the Spanish and Italian producers began to flood the market with cheap metal and used their big inventories as the basis for a price war. In November the mercury producers called a secret meeting to attempt to work out a truce between the price-cutters but no success was recorded. Price-cutting did stop in November, simply because consumers stopped buying. With prices at $85 per flask in Europe, marginal producers dropped out of the market.

In 1976 even the major producers began to cut production and/or sales, with Italy's Monte Amiata suspending operations and Spain's Almaden announcing that it would withhold all sales until prices reached 'acceptable levels'. By the end of 1977 the reduced production was much closer to matching consumption, itself now reduced by new environmental requirements in a number of countries.

It is clear that the attempts to raise prices by cartel actions foundered on the failure of the producers to make a proper estimate of demand, as well as on the moves in Europe to reduce the use of mercury for environmental reasons.

The Zircon Cartel

Rutile and zircon production has been dominated by four Australian companies since the mid-1950s. Those producers had made no attempts at collusion until the Australian government decided to encourage the cartelisation of the zircon market in February 1971 by setting minimum export prices for zircon. In response the producers agreed to stockpile zircon rather than attempt to sell it at the minimum export prices.

Zircon is produced jointly with ilmenite on the west coast of Australia and with rutile on the east coast.The demand for ilmenite and rutile increased but the demand for zircon rose much more slowly and stockpiles of zircon grew. In 1974 a technological development produced a new type of zircon refractory brick and the demand increased pushing up the price. The high price reduced the cost savings of the new brick and demand fell. This combined with the declining level of economic activity caused the price to fall.

On 6 June 1975 the Department of Minerals and Energy and the mineral sands producers announced in a press release that they would

> arrange the supply of mineral sand products in a manner that will allow a stable long-term supply of these commodities at reasonable prices commensurate with their value.

The government only approved export licences for zircon sales at A$200 per tonne or more. This high floor price discriminated against the west coast producers whose high-iron content product was only suitable for the refractory industry in which there was strong competition from a number of substitutes.

In contrast the iron-free east coast zircon had wider markets in which the competition was not as intense and they could sell their zircon at around $200 per tonne. The west coast producers wanted the price floor to be lowered to at least $130 a tonne so that their larger production plants could gain economies of scale, but the east coast producers with their smaller production plants claimed that that price level was uneconomic for them.

In early November 1975 the Australian government announced what was in effect a compromise price between the two groups, by setting minimum export prices of $140 per tonne for bulk zircon with 0.1 per cent or more iron oxide and $150 per tonne for bulk zircon with a less than 0.1 per cent iron oxide content. Demand continued to fall throughout 1976 and in November of that year the minimum export price was reduced by $25 a tonne and in March 1977 the floor prices were removed.

The failure of the cartel may be attributed first to a failure to appreciate the ability of consumers to turn to substitutes if the zircon price rose and, secondly, to a failure by the cartel members to limit output. The development of the Eneabba deposits of ilmenite are the main example of the second point.

Osborne (1976) remarks that cartels face five problems; one external and four internal. The external problem is to predict the production by non-members, while the internal problems are: to locate the contract surface (that is the profit function of the members); to choose a sharing scheme by deciding on a point on the contract surface; to establish a reliable system to detect cheating; and to provide for a reliable way of deterring members from cheating on the agreement. In an end note to his paper Osborne comments that his research into the history of cartels convinced him that a cartel is likely to survive the internal problems although it may re-form from time to time, until new substitutes appear at a price close to its marginal cost.

The strategic materials all face substitutes and because many of them are produced as by-products or co-products it is extremely difficult to establish the appropriate contract surface for a cartel and probably even more difficult to find satisfactory methods to detect or deter cheating. The attempts to establish cartels in mecury and in zircon were defeated by declines in demand as consumers turned to substitutes and by the failure of the proposed cartel members to be able to limit output effectively. Other factors that might reduce further the potential for cartel formation are the divergent aims of producers in Eastern and Western Bloc countries and the presence of government stockpiles that may be used to reduce the price of a material if it was being bid up by a cartel.

6 MARKETS AND PRICING

There are two major forms of marketing arrangements that occur in certain strategic materials as in other metals and minerals – competitive markets and producer markets. What is distinctive about the strategic materials is the combination of different types of marketing and pricing for individual materials.

In competitive markets, prices are free to move to the level that equates supply and demand. Tilton (1981, p.8) illustrates the instability that may characterise these markets (see Figure 6.1).

Figure 6.1: Competitive Markets

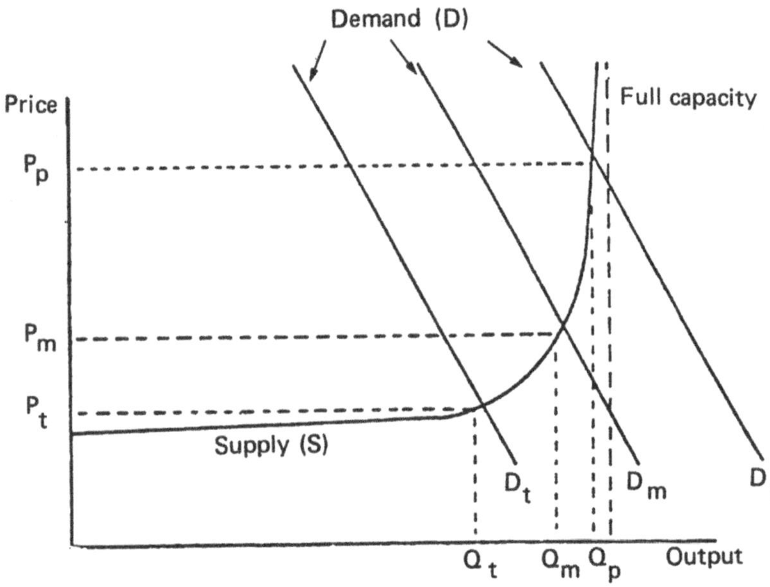

The steepness of slope of the demand and supply curves at full capacity and above reflect the inability of supply to respond to price in the short-run and the small proportion that the cost of the material has in the final goods for which it is used in most of its demand. D_t, D_m and D_p, respectively, refer to demand at the trough, midpoint and peak of the business cycle. At the peak, there is a high price but output is constrained by existing capacity with revenues and also profits quite large. Much smaller revenues and profits occur at the trough where the price and output equating supply and demand are much lower and there is idle capacity in the industry.

In producer markets where the major producers set prices, there is no allowance by producers for prices to fluctuate so as to maintain equality between short-term demand and supply. While this may have the effect of tempering, if not eliminating price instability, output and profit instability remain problems.

Figure 6.2: Producer Markets

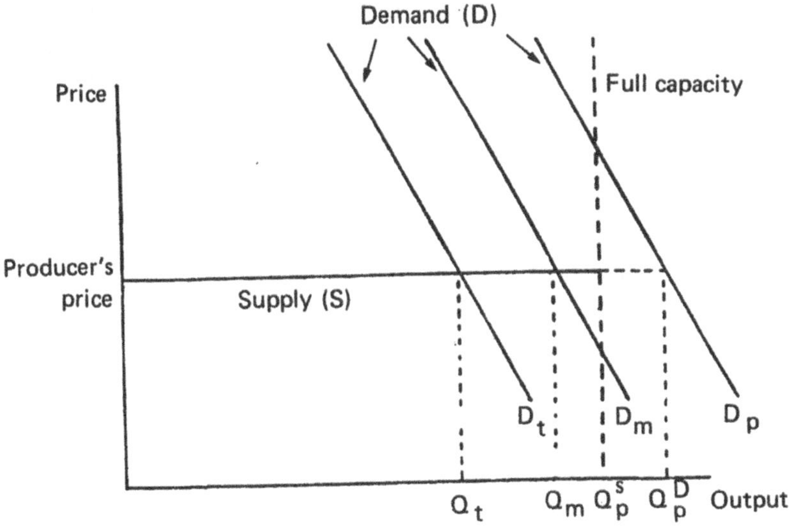

The producer market situation is illustrated in Figure 6.2 (Tilton, 1981, p.9). Even allowing the producer's price to remain completely stable, the variations in production between the full-capacity-limited peak and the trough generate considerable fluctuations in total revenues and profits. A further characteristic of producer markets is that they may have shortfalls of supply in the peak phase of the cycle because demand will exceed supply at the prevailing price and producers will ration their supplies by limiting orders and lengthening delivery times. From the viewpoint of consumers of the material, producer markets create the risk that there will be times when they will not be supplied regardless of the price they might be prepared to pay. There is, accordingly, an incentive to consumers facing producer markets to hold inventories of the product. The presence of these inventories may mean that the producer price will be unable to be increased as demand rises.

Daily spot market trading occurs in nickel, platinum and palladium and there are also futures markets for these three metals: nickel futures are traded on the London Metal Exchange and platinum futures and palladium futures are traded on the New York Mercantile Exchange.

In the absence of either a competitive market price or a producer price, a reference price is often provided by either the *Metal Bulletin* in London or the *Metal Week* or the *American Metal Market* in New York.

John Parry, the nonferrous metals editor of the *Metal Bulletin*, described the process of setting the *Metal Bulletin* price at a meeting of the Primary Tungsten Association and the International Tungsten Indicator reporting group in Stockholm in September 1979. The description appears in 14 September *Metal Bulletin*

> The day-to-day mechanics of MB's assessment is gratifyingly simple. We simply ask people what they have done. We talk to merchants, producers and consumers. We talk to people in the industry on a widespread sample basis in order to get representative information. The type of information we are concerned with is not . . . mainly inter-merchant trading. In fact the quotation would not move solely on the basis of an inter-merchant report but requires that consumers have paid prices reflected in each new quotation (p. 30).

Table 6.1 lists the main forms in which strategic materials are available and Table 6.2 summarises the main prices quoted for each of the materials. The marketing arrangements for each are described in the next section and the ways in which non-consumers may trade in strategic materials are discussed in the following section. Possible influences on the short-term price movements of three strategic materials for which monthly price data were available are explored in the final section of the chapter.

Marketing Arrangements

Antimony

There is a US producer price for antimony metal, but there is trading by New York merchants at prices that often differ markedly from the producer price. There is an active free market in antimony ore but the

Table 6.1: Main Forms in which Strategic Materials are Available

Material	Unit	Form	Packing	Quality
Antimony	5 tonnes	Ingots	Wooden cases	99.6% min. purity; 0.15% max. arsenic
Beryllium	2,500 kg	Beryllium-copper alloy	Drums	Approx. 4% beryllium content
Cadmium	2 tonnes	2 in diameter balls, sticks or ingots	Wooden cases or drums	99.95% min. purity
Chromium	1 tonne	Lumps	Steel drums	99.5% min purity
Cobalt	250 kg	Broken cathodes	Steel drums	99.5% purity
Columbium (Niobium)	2 tonnes	Ferrocolumbium	Drums	60 to 70% columbium
Germanium	20 kg	Ingots	Wooden boxes	99.99% min. purity; 50 ohm resistivity
Hafnium	100 kg	Sponge	Poly bottles	99.99% min. purity
Indium	50 kg	Ingots	Drums	99.99% min purity
Lithium	500 kg	Ingots	Watertight containers	99.99% min. purity
Manganese	10 tonnes	Ingots	Shrink-wrapped	99.8% min. purity
Electro-manganese	10 tonnes	Flakes	Steel drums	99.95% min. purity
Mercury	50 flasks	Liquid	Flasks of 76 lb	99.99% min. purity
Molybdenum	1500 kg	Molybdenum oxide powder	Tins or drums	
Nickel	lbs or tonnes	Cathode, pellet, briquette, rondelles, oxide	Drums	99.5% cathode, pellet; 75% and 90% nickel oxide
Platinum Group Metals				
Platinium	50 troy oz	Plates, ingots	Wooden boxes	99.9% min. purity (dealers); 99.95% (producers)
Palladium	100 troy oz	Ingot, sponge	Wooden boxes, bottles	99.9% min. purity
Rhodium	20 troy oz	Sponge	Plastic bottles	99.9% min. purity
Osmium	20 troy oz	Sponge	Plastic bottles	99.9% min. purity
Ruthenium	20 troy oz	Powder	Drums	99.9% min. purity
Iridium	20 troy oz	Powder	Drums	99.9% min. purity
Rhenium	lb	Metal powder	Drums	99.9% purity
Selenium	1,000 kg	Powder (–200 mesh)	Wooden cases	99.5% min. purity
Tantalite	200 lb	Ta_2O_5 ore	Bags/drums	60% Ta_2O_5

Table 6.1: Main Forms in which Strategic Materials are Available (Continued)

Material	Unit	Form	Packing	Quality
Tellurium	500 kg	Small ingots	Wooden cases	99.7% min. purity
Titanium	500 kg	Sponge (irregular granules) TG 100 brand or equivalent	Drums	99.6% typical purity
Tungsten	1 tonne	Concentrate ore	Drums	65.70% WO_3
Vanadium	2 tonnes	Ferrovanadium	Drums	78.82% vanadium
Zirconium	10 tonnes	Powdered concentrated ore	Drums	Varies with end use

Table 6.2: Main Prices Quoted for Each Strategic Material

	Producer Price	European Free Market	USA	Japan	UK	Other European	Other
Antimony	Assomet (Italy) 99.6% lire per kg	Regulus. 99.6% $ per mt in warehouse	New York dealer ¢ per lb	Yen, metric ton ex-w'house		France F per kg 99%	
Beryllium Beryl ore Beryllium Copper			$s per short ton US Be/Cu/alloy 25 $ per lb US Be-Cu/Cast ingot $per lb US Be-Cu/Mast. alloy $per lb US Rod $ per lb		Master alloy approx. 4% Be £ perks		
Cadmium	USS per lb Italy (Assomet) Lire/kg 99.95% sticks	$per lb in w'house ingots sticks	US $lb 99.95% sticks, ton lots d/d New York dealer $lb	Yen per kg ex w'house official price and market			
Chromium	Tranvaal ore Turkish ore		US electric metal US metal (9%) carbon US vacuum metal plates all $ per lb		Lump min. 99% £ per MT (5-10 lots) d/d		
Cobalt (w)	Sozacom $per lb cif USA $per lb cif	$ per lb 99.5%, in Europ. w'house	Ceramic oxide/70% Ceramic oxide/72% Fine powder/125 kg Fine powder/50 kg Metallurgical oxide MW US spot cathode			Ff per kg excl. taxes 100 kg up	Zambian $ per lb cit UK port

Table 6.2: Main Prices Quoted for Each Strategic Material (Continued)

	Producer Price	European Free Market	USA	Japan	UK	Other European	Other
			Powder Shot/cathode/250 kg				
Columbium	Canada pyrochlore		Spot columbite ore $lb US reactor ingot US reactor powder			Columbite min 65% $ per lb pentoxide content	
Germanium	US producer $kg US producer (dioxide) $kg					Zone refined 50 ohm/cm Bfr per kg cit 50 kg lots	
Indium			US ingots min 99.9% $per troy oz fob				
Lithium			US carbonate US carbonate pellet US ingot US rod all ¢s per lb				
Manganese	Assomet (Italy) Lire kg ex-works 99.5%		Ore min 48% mn cents LTU US metal/regular $lb US metal/6% N¢lb		Electro min 99.95% £ per MT ST lots d/d		
Mercury Flasks	Almaden (Spain) pp fob Spanish port $	$ min 99.99% in Eur. w'house	MW US$	Tokyo ex-w'house Yen			
Molybdenum	Climax (US) concentrate		MW dealer oxide		Powder £ per kg		

		Climax (US) oxide/cans				
Nickel		Amax briquettes	in w'house melting $per lb		LME cash LME futures	
		Western briquettes				
		Major produ-cers — cathode				
		Falconbridge ferronickel				
		Hanna ferronickel				
		SLN-FN4, ferronickel				
		Inco Sinter 1975				
		Cubaniquel				
		Assomet L/kg cathodes. 995				
	(w)	Inco melting grade cif. d/d $lb				
		Inco refined				
		Inco charged				
		Amax corrugates				
Osmium		Major producer $ troy oz		MW New York dealer	LME	Italy (Assomex) Lire pe gm 99.90%
		World producer price		NW dealer & merc. ex. futures		
		Major producer $ troy oz		MW New York dealer		
				Merc. ex. futures		
Rhenium			Powder $ per kg		Ammonium per rhenate $ per kg	
Selenium		North American producers 99.5%		MW New York dealer		

Table 6.2: Main Prices Quoted for Each Strategic Material (Continued)

	Producer Price	European Free Market	USA	Japan	UK	Other European	Other
	$lb in w'house $ per lb 100 lb lots d/d						
Tantalum	Tanco Tantalite	Ore min 60% Ta_2O_5	Spot tantalite ore				
Tellurium	Major producer slab (Asarco & Norander)				Lump and powder powder $ per lb 99/99.5% Sticks, min. 99.5% $ per lb.		
Titanium			Ore/ilmenite $ LT Ore/rutile $ST Slag $ LT Sponge $lb US bar US bullet US plate US sheet/strip	Sponge $lb	Sponge 99.3% max £ ton cit		
Tungsten	UA hydrogenred metal		US spot ore US U car metal		Powder 99.5% W £ per kg of metal		
Vanadium	Highveld, fused min. 98% V_2O_5 cif		Pentoxide/chemical $lb Pentoxide/metal $lb				
Zirconium	Ore/Australia $A per MT Ore/US $ST						

price trends there have not had a direct relation on the price for antimony metal. Approximately 16 per cent of world production comes from China which has traditionally sold almost all of its output to international merchants.

Beryllium

The ore is produced in a number of countries but there are only few producers of the metal and these (mainly US) control the very small market for the forms traded (see Table 6.1). Merchant activity is insignificant.

Cadmium

A producer price for cadmium anodes, balls and platers shapes is quoted, but dealers are often able to trade at different prices and non-North American producers tend to sell to merchants.

Chromium

Prices tend to follow the pattern set by South African producers and although direct producer-user trade is important, there is also an active free market in which large merchants trade USSR and small producers' supplies.

Cobalt

Traditionally cobalt was marketed at producer prices but the free market has become important since the disruption to Zaire's supplies.

Columbium (Niobium)

Producers, including Niobec in Canada, have set flexible prices and usually sell to consumers directly or use local agents to market their product.

Germanium

The market is tiny and producers sell directly to consumers. The only role for merchants is in mediating between central market producers and consumers. New York dealers have been able to create a free market for germanium in recent years but there is little supply for it.

Hafnium

Producers sell directly to consumers.

Indium

The prices have usually been set by the North American producers who sell directly to large consumers. Other producers sell at a discount or a premium on these prices to smaller consumers. Supplies from the USSR, Japan and Latin America are traded through international merchants.

Lithium

Producers are the main influence on prices. Merchants trade the sporadic USSR supplies.

Manganese

The largest producers have a producer price, but there is also a free market in which small producers and merchants trade. Merchants and smaller consumers also have created an active, if small, market in ferro-mananese.

Mercury

The failure of the mercury producers to set effective producer prices is discussed in Chapter 5. Sales are mainly at free market prices. Consumers have had more influence on market prices here than in most other materials.

Molybdenum

Climax Molybdenum Co., the USA's largest producer, sets producer prices for concentrate and for molybdic oxide in cans. Dealer prices have been higher or lower than the producer prices in recent years. There are a few international merchants who specialise in the refractory metals, including molybdenum.

Nickel

Inco Ltd has traditionally been the leader in the setting of producer prices and for most of 1979 and 1980 the major producers adhered to a uniform pricing policy. Discounts started to be made in late 1980. There is an active free market and a small futures market.

Platinum

The varying importance of spot and futures markets for materials where there are a few major producers is best shown by the case of platinum in the mid-1960s and again in the early 1980s. In the mid-1960s there were three main platinum producers: Rustenburg Platinum Mines

Limited of South Africa which set a producer price, Inco Limited of Canada and the USSR. Engelhard Minerals and Chemicals Corporation acted as sole selling agents for Inco and also sold some of Rustenburg's output, with Johnson Mattley and Co. Ltd the sole sellers for the rest of Rustenburg's output and Almazjurelirexport, the Soviet marketing agency, sold the USSR's production. Engelhard and Johnson Mattley were both major fabricators of platinum but they also sold to other fabricators and to end users,while the Russians sold refined products. The former used Rustenburg's producer price but Almazjurelirexport sold at what the market would bear. In addition, there existed a free market in physical platinum operated by dealers in London, New York, Zurich, Germany and Japan. The free market catered for consumer shortfalls and excess inventories and provided an outlet for recovered scrap. The New York Mercantile Exchange (Nymex) offered futures trading in platinum. Owing to the South African exchange control regulations, Rustenburg was unable to trade in futures markets and the consistent and vocal opposition by Inco to a new futures contract for another of the metals it produces (nickel) suggests that it probably did not participate. Dealers in the free market and consumers of platinum could, and did, use the futures market for hedging purposes and there were sufficient speculators and arbitrageurs to ensure a continuous market.

In a recent paper, Ian Grieg (1981), former chairman of Impala Platinum Ltd, discussed the changes that occurred in the platinum market in the 1970s and in 1980. First, two more primary producers entered the market, Impala Platinum Ltd and Western Platinum Mines Ltd, both South African. Secondly, the new demand for platinum for use in catalytic converters by the automobile industry (which accounted for over 25 per cent of Western world consumption in 1979) led to special contractual arrangements being made between the platinum producers and the automobile industry that were outside the existing market mechanisms. Thirdly, in 1979 the speculative spillover from the gold and silver markets into platinum (as well as other commodity) markets pushed the free market and futures market prices for platinum to more than double the producer price. In these circumstances, neither dealers nor consumers were able to use the free and futures markets for hedging and dealers were short of working capital as consumers were short of inventories. On 20 December 1979, platinum futures trade represented 242,900 ounces of platinum or 27 per cent of the 1979 production of all platinum group metals.

While Grieg's view of the recent excesses of the free and futures markets for platinum is representative of the views held by producers of this and the other metals for which free market and futures trading also exist, it is possible to find a useful role for them. The interests of many consumers were protected during the high free and futures market prices by the maintaining of the producer price at much lower levels, leaving dealers, marginal consumers and marginal inventory changes for consumers with long-run contracts, investors and others to the free and futures markets.

Rhenium

A European free market and a UK price are quoted.

Selenium

There is a commercial grade selenium traded in the European free market, but the high purity selenium which is in growing demand is not able to be traded on the free market because of its technical specifications. A more serious reduction in the scope of the free market for selenium was pointed out by the *Metal Bulletin* (12 April 1979, p. 24 and 5 June 1979, pp. 24-5) which noted Mitsubishi Metal Corporation's appointment of Sassoon and Co. as their selenium distributor and adviser in Continental Europe for exports that may be of the order of 15 tonnes per month. Previously when the company's production for export was at lower levels, it had usually been sold on the free market. In the *Metal Bulletin*'s view, demand trends towards high priority selenium in combination with Mitsubishi's new strategy would reduce the effectiveness of the free market.

Tantalite

Producers and consumers of tantalite have expressed doubts in the past few years about the ability of the free market price to reflect the true production position. Producers in particular have been concerned that sharp increases in prices would lead to widespread substitution by consumers.

In fact, the free market for tantalite has had a much narrower base than might appear at first glance, if the destination of the output of the various producers is examined. That part of world tantalite production recovered from tin-slags at smelters in Malaysia and Thailand is usually sold on long-term contracts related to the free market quotation published by the London *Metal Bulletin*.

Canada's only tantalum producer is the largest purely tantalum mine in the Western world, Tantalum Corporation of Canada's (Tanco)

Bernic Lake mine. Tanco is the only producer to publish a fixed producer price.

Of the African producers, Mozambique's output is mainly directed to Communist countries (although it appears to go through Western merchants to get there) while Nigeria and Zaire normally sell on a long-term contract basis and only occasionally have small lots to place on the free market.

The Australian producer, Greenbushes, refers in its 1981 annual report to selling direct to consumers. It appears that perhaps less than 10 per cent of annual production is disposed of on the free market and it would not be surprising if the price determined there was less than representative of total demand and supply.

Tellurium

A very small market with prices mostly fixed by producers who sell directly to consumers. State-owned corporation trading occurs on a free market basis.

Titanium

Producers mainly control prices, although there is a small free market. There is a market for scrap titanium.

Tungsten

The *Metal Bulletin* of 4 September 1979 described tungsten pricing as a

> chaotic mixture of part producer pricing, free market oligopolies, massive East Bloc buying patterns and the new consumer consensus on stable price indexation.

In April 1978 the Primary Tungsten Association announced the establishment of the International Tungsten Indicator (ITI) as a new system of fixing the price of tungsten concentrates. Data used in this indicator comprised only primary producer and tungsten concentrate consumer prices. The ITI has been published twice monthly since July 1978.

While the ITI was established because the Primary Tungsten Association alleged that the *Metal Bulletin* price included information from tungsten dealers in its compilation and might produce a different price to that derived solely from producer-consumer transactions, the difference between the average ITI price and the average of the *Metal Bulletin* monthly averages was only 11 cents ($US140.54 to $US140.65).

In the present author's view the *Metal Bulletin* (14 September 1979, p. 30) has quite fairly commented that

> The structure of the ITI, using mainly long-term fixed price contracts and formula priced contracts as inputs (in addition to occasional spot business reports) introduces, we contend, an historical bias to the resulting figure. We believe that when the ITI was formed its designers missed an opportunity to create an almost ideal price indicator. Instead they chose to sacrifice this ambition in favour of an indicator whose primary quality was stability, not reality.

Vanadium

Official producer prices are used for most long-term consumer contracts. In times of excess demand, merchants are sometimes influential in bidding up free market prices to premium levels.

Zirconium

Direct producer-consumer sales used to exhaust the whole market but the attempt to establish a zircon cartel (see Chapter 5) lead to the growth of a free market at less than producer prices.

Market Manipulation

The London minor metal market has been a focus for trade in a number of the strategic materials. When the Minor Metals Traders Association was founded in London in 1973 antimony, cadmium, mercury, nickel and selenium were classified as minor metals and most other strategic materials were included when the classification was broadened substantially in 1977. Alan Wye (1982), in a discussion of the development of minor metal trading in London since 1969, refers to various techniques used to influence the market in minor metals in the period 1970 to 1976, among them buying or selling the market up or down and selective operations. The latter technique involved a trader offering or bidding for material from the companies least likely to buy or sell to him in order to spread word of his interest. Bigger operators would begin to contact the trader and he could buy or sell to them, or if his objective was to move the price he might tell a seller that he could get a high price for a lot much larger than the normal trading list or tell a buyer that he could have the metal at a low price if he bought a lot much larger than the normal trading lot. Another strategy mentioned by Wye as being used in this period was the taking of a joint position by a group of traders in order to push the market in a desired direction.

The steep decline in prices from October 1976 into 1977 had the effect, in Wye's opinion, of reducing substantially the manipulative element in the trade. Although several individual metals such as cobalt and molybdenum in 1979-80 and germanium from 1980 have seen major market imbalances since 1977. Wye suggests that this has not been evidence of significant manipulation in the markets.

The markets for a number of the strategic materials are very small, however, and with the increased holdings of stockpiles by governments and of reserves by private sector strategic material funds there is a danger that these markets will become very narrow and more easily manipulated.

Trading in Strategic Materials

For individual investors who are neither producers nor consumers, purchases of strategic materials may be made through commodity brokers and dealers. The potential investor would be well advised to examine the past experience and present status of the free market before becoming heavily committed in a particular material in order to ensure that a sale at realistic prices will be possible when a realisation of the investment is required. At present, nickel, platinum and palladium are the only strategic materials for which daily spot and futures prices are quoted. The *Metal Bulletin* (London) the *American Metal Market* and *Metal Week* (New York) provide price information on a regular basis for the strategic materials.

Assistance might also be sought from the Minor Metal Traders Association of London which was formally created in 1973 'to encourage, participate in, and foster the activities of traders in minor metals with a view to maintenance of good trade practices, healthy competition and the reputation of such traders on the basis of sound commercial principles'. There are some 40 UK members and a further 13 overseas. The Association has devised a contract form (which a sub-committee is presently revising) and regularly visits UK and Continental warehouses to investigate conditions.

A second form in which investors might take an interest in strategic materials is in the several strategic metal funds at present being marketed in the US and the USA with investments ranging from $500 each to index-linked bonds. The difficulty that the presence of these funds threatens is that they create off-market inventories that are unrelated to either production or consumption and sales from them may be sufficient to disrupt the comparatively small markets in a number of these metals.

For the present, the safest vehicle for individual investment in strategic materials appears to be shares in the miners, explorers and producers of strategic materials. The operating mines in the Western world that produce strategic materials are listed in Appendix 2.

Influences on Short-term Price Movements: Some Explorations

It may be seen from Chapter 3 that world production figures for the majority, if not all, of the strategic materials cannot be estimated precisely and this inhbits the development of appropriate economic models to estimate prices. Not all of the strategic materials are subject to short-term price movement: for example, lithium producers sell direct to consumers and the price of lithium ingot pegged at $US19-$US20 per lb on 15 October 1980 still prevailed in August 1982. On the other hand, platinum, which has a producer price, is also traded on a daily basis on the New York Mercantile Exchnge. In this section the possible influences on the short-term price movements of two of the strategic materials – antimony and platinum – will be explored. The main purpose of this exploration is to discover whether these prices may be influenced by, or associated with, the level of business activity, political tension or short-run interest rates or prices.

Following Granger (1969) and Sims (1972) the relationships between the monthly prices of antimony and of platinum and the variables listed in Appendices 6.1 and 6.2 are explored, in terms of predictability according to price information. Pierce and Haugh (1979) define this approach as follows:

> a variable X causes another variable Y, with respect to a given universe or information set that includes X and Y, if present Y can be better predicted by using past values of X than by not doing so, all other information contained in the past of the universe, being used in either case (p. 266).

The Granger method which is used here implies that if Y is not caused by X, then lagged values of X should not aid in the prediction of Y once the past history of Y has been taken into account. Accordingly, if Y is regressed on its own lagged values and the lagged values of X, the latter variables ought not to be statistically significant. It has become usual to refer to these tests as 'Granger-causality' tests in order to distinguish them as a means of identifying temporal correlation of two series.

Zellner (1979) summarises the main criticisms of these causality tests as follows:

> The mechanical application of causality tests is an extreme form of 'measurement without theory' perhaps motivated by the hope that application of statistical techniques without the delicate and difficult work of integrating statistical techniques and subject matter considerations will be able to produce useful and dependable results.

The purpose of the application of causality tests in this chapter is simply to provide information about the possible influences on the prices of the two strategic materials under discussion. It has long been recognised that regression analyses yielding high values of R^2 may often be obtained even when there is no underlying relationship between the dependent and the explanatory variables. Using the lagged values of the dependent variable in Granger-causality tests has the effect of detrending the series and therefore reducing the probability of finding a relationship between two variables that merely move up or down together over time and are not really causally related.

To the extent that each of the strategic materials, whose price series is used here, may be regarded as a representative strategic material there are certain hypotheses that may be advanced. Each of these will be briefly examined in turn. Following Harvey (1980) levels rather than first differences are used.

The US Money Supply (M_3) (UMS)

The association hypothesised between the US money supply and a representative strategic material is that an increasing US money supply is consistent with an expanding growth of national output which would increase the demand for strategic materials used in industry. Since the supply of strategic matefials is inelastic in the short-run any increase in demand ought to be reflected in rising prices.

The US Treasury Bill Rate (UTB)

When interest rates are low, the demand for strategic materials for use in industrial production should increase and, as the opportunity cost of holding strategic materials is low, investors and consumers may be interested in stockpiling them. At high interest rates, declining industrial production implies declining demand for strategic materials and investors and consumers find the opportunity cost of stockpiling strategic materials too exenpsive a policy. A negative association between the T-bill rate and the price of a representative strategic material would be expected.

The US Discount Rate (UDR) and the *US Long-term Bond Rate* (ULT) are used to explore the possibility that these other interest rates may be more appropriate.

The US Consumer Price Index (USCPI) is used to represent the inflation rate. As strategic materials are real assets, an increase in the (USCPI) might be expected to increase interest in real as opposed to money assets.

The US Industrial Production Index (USIP)

It would be expected that the price of a representative strategic material would vary consistently in response to the US Industrial Production Index due to the high proportion of strategic materials used in industrial production in the United States.

The Saudi Arabia Oil Price (SOP)

In response to the movements in the Saudi oil price during the 1970s changes occurred within the industrial structure of a number of economies in an endeavour to economise on the use of oil. It might be expected that the oil price might have been an influence on the prices of strategic materials.

The Hudson Political Tension Index (PTI)

The 'strategic' uses of strategic materials would lead us to expect the price of a representative strategic material to react to political tension. The Hudson Political Tension Index is developed in three stages: first, those political, economic, military and other events likely to affect global political tension were identified and listed on a monthly basis over the 1971 to 1980 period; secondly, the impact of each individual event on the level of international tension was evaluated and the event was weighted; thirdly, the weights of the individual events were totalled to derive a monthly cumulative level of international political tension.

The results of the regressions run using platinum suggests that the platinum price is responsive to the US money supply, to the US Consumer Price Index and to the US Industrial Production Index.

This supports the view that industrial demand is a major determinant of the price of platinum. While the analysis does not extend to examining all the potential influences on the platinum price, influences emanating from industrial demand and the past price of platinum are sufficient to account for its price movement.

Appendix 6.2 reports the regression results for antimony. Neither the equations nor the variables used produce as useful results as those for platinum. Only the US Consumer Price Index and the US Industrial Production appear to have any causal influence on the antimony price.

From the results reported in the appendices the inference can be drawn that the prices of both metals are influenced by industrial demand but that the Political Tension Index has no influence and neither do interest rates nor the price of oil.

Appendix 6.1: Platinum, Monthly December 1975 to December 1981

$$\text{IA } P1 = 136.330 + 1.312P1_{t-1} - 0.235P1_{t-2} + 0.079P1_{t-3} - 1.638UMS_{t-1} + 0.350UMS_t$$

$(11.21)^{xxxx}$ $(0.07)^{xxxx}$ (-0.97) (0.48) $(-5.77)^{xxxx}$ (0.93)

$$+ 0.020UMS_{t-3}$$

(0.07)

$R^2 = .990$ $F = 1151$

$$\text{IB } UMS = 102.073 + C.129P1_{t-1} + 0.001P1_{t-2} - 0.007P1_{t-3} - 0.076UMS_{t-1}$$

$(23.97)^{xxxx}$ $(2.26)^{x}$ (0.010) (-0.12) (-0.77)

$$+ 0.003UMS_{t-2} + 0.094UMS_{t-3}$$

(0.02) (1.06)

$R^2 = .932$ $F = 166$

$$\text{2A } P1 = 26.882 + 1.049P1_{t-1} - 0.120PL_{t-2} + 0.188P1_{t-3} - 5.126UDR_{t-1}$$

$(3.44)^{xxx}$ $(4.74)^{xxxx}$ (-0.36) (0.83) (-0.87)

$$+ 2.365UDR_{t-2} - 3.456UDR_{t-3}$$

(0.28) (-0.59)

$R^2 = .974$ $F = 456$

$$\text{2B } UDR = 1.226 - 0.003P1_{t-1} + 0.008P1_{t-2} + 0.005P1_{t-3} + 0.872UDR_{t-1}$$

$(4.17)^{xxxx}$ (-0.43) (0.71) (0.61) $(3.93)^{xxx}$

$$- 0.155UDR_{t-2} - 0.188UDR_{t-3}$$

(-0.49) (-0.85)

$R^2 = .944$ $F = 203$

$$\text{3A } P1 = 64.400 + 0.916P1_{t-1} - 0.172P1_{t-2} + 0.456P1_{t-3}$$

$(6.30)^{xxxx}$ $(5.30)^{xxxx}$ (-0.68) $(2.42)^{x}$

$$- 6.676ULT_{t-1} + 3.969ULT_{t-2} - 9.810ULT_{t-3}$$

$(-1.68)^{-}$ (0.70) $(-2.28)^{x}$

$R^2 = .981$ $F = 622$

$$\text{3B } ULT = 2.755 - 0{,}004P1_{t-1} + 0.007P1_{t-}{}^{2} + 0.007P1_{t-3}$$

$(5.95)^{xxxx}$ (-0.630) (0.66) (0.85)

$$+ 0.728ULT_{t-1} - 0.174ULT_{t-2} - 0.144ULT_{t-3}$$

$R^2 = .900$ $F = 109$

$$\text{4A } P1 = 20.599 + 0.937P1_{t-1} - 0.069P1_{t-2} + 0.177P1_{t-3}$$

$(3.24)^{xx}$ $(6.62)^{xxx}$ (-0.35) (1.20)

$$-1.348UTB_{t-1} + 1.500UTB_{t-2} - 3.241UTB_{t-3}$$

(-0.50) (0.40) (-1.43)

$R^2 = .974$ $F = 451$

$$\text{4B } UTB = 0.781 - 0.006P1_{t-1} + 0.022P1_{t-2} - 0.006P1_{t-3} + 1.052UTB_{t-1}$$

$(2.32)^{x}$ (-0.80) $(2.19)^{x}$ (0.80) $(7.36)^{xxxx}$

$$- 0.573UTB_{t-2} + 0.084UTB_{t-3}$$

$(2.88)^{xx}$ (0.56)

$R^2 = .912$ $F = 126$

$$5A\quad P1 = 134.492 + 1.149P1_{t-1} - 0.168P1_{t-2} + 0.292P1_{t-3} - 1.107YSCP1_{t-1}$$
$$(12.10)^{xxxx}\quad (7.29)^{xxxx}\quad (0.71)\quad (1.83)^{-}\quad (-5.26)^{xxxx}$$
$$+ 0.183USCPI_{t-2} - 0.227USCPI_{t-3}$$
$$(0.63)\quad (-1.16)$$
$$R^2 = .990 \quad F = 1272$$

$$5B\quad USCPI = 119.747 + 0.022P1_{t-1} - 0.014PL_{t-2} + 0.245P1_{t-3} + 0.135USCPI_{t-1}$$
$$(18.57)^{xxxx}\quad (0.24)\quad (-0.10)\quad (2.65)^{x}\quad (1.11)$$
$$+ 0.020USCPI_{t-2} - 0.212USCPI_{t-3}$$
$$(0.12)\quad (-1.87)$$
$$R^2 = .950 \quad F = 230$$

$$6A\quad P1 = 20.838 + 0.831P1_{t-1} - 0.053P1_{t-2} + 0.255P1_{t-3} + 0.869SOP_{t-1}$$
$$(3.33)^{xx}\quad (4.73)^{xxxx}\quad (-0.22)\quad (1.44)\quad (0.41)$$
$$+ 0.587SOP_{t-2} - 2.707SOP_{t-3}$$
$$(0.21)\quad (-1.27)$$
$$R^2 = .974 \quad F = 460$$

$$6B\quad SOP = 0.982 - 0.005P1_{t-1} + 0.013P1_{t-2} - 0.003 + 0.924SOP_{t-1}$$
$$(1.083)^{-}\quad (-0.34)\quad (0.69)\quad (-0.23)\quad (5.16)^{xxxx}$$
$$- 0.068SOP_{t-2} + 0.035SOP_{t-3}$$
$$(-0.28)\quad (0.19)$$
$$R^2 = .957 \quad F = 274$$

$$7A\quad P1 = 18.776 + 0.900P1_{t-1} - 0.014PL_{t-2} + 0.106P1_{t-3} + 0.396EDL_{t-1}$$
$$(2.98)^{xx}\quad (6.31)^{xxxx}\quad (-0.07)\quad (0.73)\quad (0.18)$$
$$- 0.299EDL_{t-2} - 0.980EDL_{t-3}$$
$$(-0.10)\quad (-0.42)$$
$$R^2 = .973 \quad F = 440$$

$$7B\quad EDL = 0.688 - 0.002P1_{t-1} + 0.027P1_{t-2} - 0.009P1_{t-3} + 0.986EDL_{t-1}$$
$$(1.63)\quad (-0.31)\quad (2.31)^{x}\quad (-0.99)\quad (6.87)^{xxxx}$$
$$- 0.525EDL_{t-2} + 0.050EDL_{t-3}$$
$$(-2.64)^{x}\quad (0.32)$$
$$R^2 = .908 \quad F = 119$$

$$8A\quad P1 = 140.57 + 1.300P1_{t-1} - 0.162P1_{t-2} - 0.092P1_{t-3} - 1.520USIP_{t-1}$$
$$(12.20)^{xxxx}\quad (8.10)^{xxxx}\quad (-0.68)\quad (-0.57)\quad (-6.03)^{xxxx}$$
$$+ 0.230USIP_{t-2} + 0.238USIP_{t-3}$$
$$(0.68)\quad (1.04)$$
$$R^2 = .990 \quad F = 1290$$

$$8B\quad USIP = 112.81 + 0.141P1_{t-1} + 0.014P1_{t-2} - 0.119P1_{t-3}$$
$$(25.22)^{xxxx}\quad (2.26)^{x}\quad (0.15)\quad (-1.91)^{-}$$
$$- 0.078USIP_{t-1} + 0.001USIP_{t-2} + 0.210USIP_{t-3}$$
$$(-0.80)\quad (0.01)\quad (2.37)^{x}$$
$$R^2 = .705 \quad F = 29.78$$

9A $$PI = 28.05 + 0.917PI_{t-1} - 0.004PI_{t-2} + 0.084PI_{t-3}$$
$$(3.63)^{xxx} \quad (7.05)^{xxxx} \quad (-0.02) \quad (0.67)$$
$$- 0.161PTI_{t-1} - 0.181PTI_{t-2} - 0.245PTI_{t-3}$$
$$(-0.76) \quad (-0.84) \quad (-1.21)$$
$R^2 = .974 \quad F = 463$

9B $$PTI = 18.75 - 0.056PI_{t-1} + 0.121PI_{t-2} - 0.020PI_{t-3} + 0.188PTI_{t-1}$$
$$(3.93)^{xxx} \quad (-0.70) \quad (1.09) \quad (-0.26) \quad (1.44)$$
$$+ 0.0006PTI_{t-2} - 0.083PTI_{t-3}$$
$$(0.005) \quad (-0.67)$$
$R^2 = .201 \quad F = 4$

Appendix 6.2: Antimony Monthly, December 1975 to December 1981

1C $$ANT = 121.894 + 0.173ANT_{t-1} + 0.504ANT_{t-2} - 0.877ANT_{t-3} + 0.074UMS_{t-1}$$
$$(14.74)^{xxxx} \quad (0.36) \quad (0.64) \quad (-1.87) \quad (0.11)$$
$$-0.708UMS_{t-2} + 1.356UMS_{t-3}$$
$$(-0.63) \quad (2.07)^{x}$$
$R^2 = .628 \quad F = 21.28$

1D $$UMS = 84.653 - 0.954ANT_{t-1} + 0.903ANT_{t-2} - 0.760ANT_{t-3} + 1.602UMS_{t-1}$$
$$(13.83)^{xxxx} \quad (-2.740)^{xx} \quad (1.572) \quad (-2.18)^{x} \quad (3.29)^{xx}$$
$$-1.288UMS_{t-2} + 1.160UMS_{t-3}$$
$$(-1.37) \quad (2.34)$$
$R^2 = .831 \quad F = 60.32$

2C $$ANT = 139.634 + 0.069ANT_{t-1} + 0.049ANT_{t-2} - 0.046ANT_{t-3}$$
$$(20.98)^{xxxx} \quad (0.68) \quad (0.34) \quad (-0.50)$$
$$+ 1.522UDR_{t-1} - 1.148UDR_{t-2} + 3.333UDR_{t-3}$$
$$(0.71) \quad (-0.33) \quad (1.56)$$
$R^2 = .791 \quad F = 46$

2D $$UDR = 4.908 - 0.046ANT_{t-1} + 0.013ANT_{t-2} + 0.002ANT_{t-2} + 1.334UDR_{t-1}$$
$$(9.65)^{xxxx} \quad (-5.98)^{xxxx} \quad (1.17) \quad (0.29) \quad (8.23)^{xxxx}$$
$$-0.245UDR_{t-2} + 0.015UDR_{t-3}$$
$$(-0.94) \quad (0.09)$$
$R^2 = .970 \quad F = 402$

3C $$ANT = 126.141 + 0.088 ANT_{t-1} + 0.111ANT_{t-2} - 0.057ANT_{t-3} + 2.782ULT_{t-1}$$
$$(15.47)^{xxxx} \quad (0.62) \quad (0.52) \quad (-0.38)$$
$$-2.379ULT_{t-2} + 3.192ULT_{t-3}$$
$$(-0.53) \quad (1.04)$$
$R^2 = 653 \quad F = 23.67$

3D $$ULT = 5.355 - 0.054ANT_{t-1} + 0.034ANT_{t-2} - 0.016ANT_{t-3} + 1.443ULT_{t-1}$$
$$(9.68)^{xxxx} \quad (-5.66)^{xxxx} \quad (2.38)^{x} \quad (-1.60) \quad (8.16)^{xxxx}$$
$$-0.748ULT_{t-2} + 0.457ULT_{t-3}$$
$$(-2.49)^{x} \quad (2.20)^{x}$$
$R^2 = .936 \quad F = 178$

$$
\begin{array}{llllll}
\text{4C} & ANT = 135.010 & + 0.093ANT_{t-1} & + 0.044ANT_{t-2} & + 0.003ANT_{t-3} & \\
 & (18.64)^{xxxx} & (1.22) & (0.50) & (0.06) & \\
 & + 1.802UTB_{t-1} & - 1.075UTB_{t-2} & + 2.084UTB_{t-3} & & \\
 & (1.86) & (-0.69) & (2.05)^{x} & & R^2 = .744 \quad F = 35.92
\end{array}
$$

$$
\begin{array}{lllllll}
\text{4D} & UTB = 3.96 & - 0.041ANT_{t-1} & + 0.027ANT_{t-2} & - 0.007ANT_{t-3} & + 1.388UTB_{t-1} & \\
 & (4.08)^{xxx} & (-4.05)^{xxx} & (2.30)^{x} & (-0.88) & (10.69)^{xxxx} & \\
 & - 0.700UTB_{t-2} & + 0.328UTB_{t-3} & & & & \\
 & (-3.38)^{xx} & (2.41)^{x} & & & & R^2 = .915 \quad F = 130
\end{array}
$$

$$
\begin{array}{llllll}
\text{5C} & ANT = 126.637 & + 0.264ANT_{t-1} & + 0.032ANT_{t-2} & - 0.339ANT_{t-3} & \\
 & (15.73)^{xxxx} & (0.66) & (0.05) & (-0.83) & \\
 & -0.067UCP_{t-1} & - 0.031UCP_{t-2} & + 0.470UCP_{t-3} & & \\
 & (-0.15) & (-0.04) & (1.02) & & R^2 = .663 \quad F = 24.64
\end{array}
$$

$$
\begin{array}{llllll}
 & UCP = 11-.60 & - 0.818ANT_{t-1} & + 0.169ANT_{t-2} & - 0.267ANT_{t-3} & \\
 & (14.46)^{xxxx} & (3.41)^{x} & (0.29) & (-0.69) & \\
 & + 1.14UCP_{t-1} & - 0.193UCP_{t-2} & + 0.379UCP_{t-3} & & \\
 & (2.74)^{xx} & (-0.29) & (0.87) & & R^2 = .925 \quad F = 150
\end{array}
$$

$$
\begin{array}{llllll}
\text{6C} & ANT = 131.952 & + 0.002ANT_{t-1} & - 0.006ANT_{t-2} & + 0.195ANT_{t-3} & \\
 & (16.99)^{xxxx} & (0.02) & (-0.05) & (1.97) & \\
 & + 2.341SOP_{t-1} & + 0.074SOP_{t-2} & - 1.475SOP_{t-3} & & \\
 & (2.17)^{x} & (0.05) & (-1.35) & & R^2 = .701 \quad F = 29.25
\end{array}
$$

$$
\begin{array}{llllll}
\text{6D} & SOP = 8.995 & - 0.060ANT_{t-1} & - 0.013ANT_{t-2} & + 0.020ANT_{t-3} & \\
 & (7.43)^{xxxx} & (3.41)^{xx} & (-0.67) & (1.30) & \\
 & + 1.069SOP_{t-1} & + 0.168SOP_{t-2} & - 0.166SOP_{t-3} & & \\
 & (6.38)^{xxxx} & (0.75) & (-0.97) & & R^2 = .974 \quad F = 468
\end{array}
$$

$$
\begin{array}{llllll}
\text{7C} & ANT = 135.873 & + 0.092\ ANT_{t-1} & + 0.047ANT_{t-2} & + 0.001ANT_{t-3} & \\
 & (19.00)^{xxxx} & (1.25) & (0.55) & (0.02) & \\
 & + 1.454EDL_{t-1} & - 0.896_{t-2} & + 1.743CDL_{t-3} & & \\
 & (1.93) & (-0.74) & (2.21)^{x} & & R^2 = .752 \quad F = 37.46
\end{array}
$$

$$
\begin{array}{llllll}
\text{7D} & EDL = 4.477 & - 0.047ANT_{t-1} & + 0.034ANT_{t-2} & - 0.010ANT_{t-3} & \\
 & (3.51)^{xxx} & (-3.61)^{xxx} & (2.23)^{x} & (-0.96) & \\
 & + 1.33EDL_{t-1} & - 0.648EDL_{t-2} & + 0.333EDL_{t-3} & & \\
 & (9.97)^{xxxx} & (-3.03)^{xx} & (2.31)^{x} & & R^2 = .905 \quad F = 116
\end{array}
$$

8C $ANT = 130.676 + 1.313ANT_{t-1} - 0.426ANT_{t-2} + 0.132ANT_{t-3}$
(16.50)xxxx (3.74)xxx (-0.75) (0.37)
$-1.475USIP_{t-1} + 0.581USIP_{t-2} - 0.036USIP_{t-3}$
(-3.20)xx (0.78) (-0.07) $R^2 = 688$ $F = 27.52$

8D $USIP = 102.54 - 0.041ANT_{t-1} + 0.076ANT_{t-2} + 0.036ANT_{t-3}$
(17.82)xxxx (-0.16) (0.18) (0.14)
$+ 0.234USIP_{t-1} - 0.083USIP_{t-2} + 0.044USIP_{t-3}$
(0.70) (-0.15) (0.13) $R^2 = .461$ $F = 11.27$

9C $ANT = 113.319 + 0.269ANT_{t-1} - 0.021ANT_{t-2} + 0.92ANT_{t-3} + 0.052PTI_{t-1}$
(12.79)xxxx (2.95)xx (-0.21) (1.29) (0.50)
$+ 0.129PTI_{t-2} + 0.109PTI_{t-3}$
(1.20) (1.05) $R^2 = .540$ $F = 15.08$

$PTI = 25.862 - 0.126ANT_{t-1} + 0.037ANT_{t-2} + 0.048ANT_{t-3}$
(2.38)x (-1.13) (-.30) (0.55)
$+ 0.301PTI_{t-1} + 0.159PTI_{t-2} + 0.040PTI_{t-3}$
(2.35) (1.21) (0.31) $R^2 = 0.111$ $F = 2.50$

If P exceeds 10%	BLANK
If P is significant at 10% and not 5%	-
If P is significant at 5% but not 1%	x
If P is significant at 1% but not 0.1%	xx
If P is significant at 0.1% but not 0.01%	xxx
If P is significant at 0.01% or better	xxxx

7 CONCLUSION

There is no real consensus on the ambit of strategic materials, but however they are defined, for the major industrialised nations at least, several of them could cause a crisis situation if supply was disrupted for even a short period. The possibility of a supply disruption being caused by political events in a major producing country is the risk aspect usually emphasised in studies of strategic materials.

Chapter 1 examined the importance of South Africa as a source of supply of several strategic materials to a number of countries and considered the vulnerability of the USA, and the UK, France, West Germany and Canada with respect to their import reliance for strategic material supplies. A further aspect of supply noted in this chapter was the dependence of the production of many strategic materials on the primary production of other metals.

Chapter 2 discussed the range of existing and potential uses of each of the strategic materials while Chapter 3 identified their major sources of supply. In Chapter 4 the focus was on the extent to which supplies of the individual strategic materials could be stretched by substitution or by recycling. Only antimony and germanium have a high level of recycling although some extension of the supplies of other materials through recycling may be possible. Beryllium, hafnium, mercury, the platinum group metals and titanium (in some uses) do not have ready substitutes and only the platinum group metals of that list could have their supply stretched by recycling. Manganese, cobalt and molybdenum may be accessed through deep-ocean nodules but failing that development, they also do not have ready substitutes or can be significantly recycled.

Chapter 5 examined the possibilities of supply disruptions or restriction occurring for each of the strategic materials. Beryllium, cobalt, columbium and, possibly, manganese appear to be the most vulnerable to these disruptions but as is noted in the second section of the chapter estimating the possibility of supply disruptions through political risk estimates is problematic. Environmental considerations and regulations are potentially disruptive threats to supply and stockpiling, although their purpose is to protect against supply disruptions. In the last section of chapter 5 the often-mentioned possibility of cartels is discussed but it is concluded that the conditions for the successful establishment of a cartel do not appear to exist in strategic materials.

Chapter 6 examined the aspects of markets and pricing which are usually neglected in discussions of strategic materials. From the discussion of the individual marketing arrangements it is clear that several of the strategic materials have small, narrow markets and with stockpiling by governments and the possibility of private sector strategic material funds holding reserves of strategic materials, these markets may be even further reduced and more able to be manipulated. Forms of market manipulation that have been used in these markets are discussed briefly in this chapter. The final section of Chapter 6 reported the results of an investigation of possible short-run influences on the prices of two strategic materials for which monthly prices are available – antimony and platinum. The US Industrial Production Index is the only variable tested to be significant for antimony and platinum. For platinum, industrial demand and the past price of platinum are sufficient to account for its price movement. The results are less useful for antimony, where only the US Consumer Price Index and the US Industrial Production Index appear to have any causal influence on its price.

Risk Aspects of Strategic Materials

In conclusion the risk aspects of the strategic materials discussed in this book are summarised below. A classification of the materials into risk groups is made at the end of that summary.

Antimony

In ample supply with recycling important from several uses, antimony is facing declining demand in its most important use. There is an active market for antimony ore and merchant and producer trading in antimony metal.

Beryllium

Its most important use is beryllium metal as an alloy, especially with copper, but as an oxide, a metal and an alloy it has a wide range of uses in the defence industry in the nuclear field and in ceramics. The USSR and the USA are the only important producers although a number of other countries have small-scale production or reserves. There are few feasible substitutes for beryllium in its main uses and no recycling occurs. There is only a very small market and little incentive for new producers to develop reserves.

Cadmium

Derived entirely as a by-product of zinc smelting and refining, cadmium has important uses in protecting iron and steel products from oxidation. The estimated reserve base of cadmium in the free world appears to be sufficient to sustain existing levels of production well into the next century. Both producers and dealers trade in cadmium.

Chromium

With the reduction in required chromium content for ores used in oxygen decarburisation processes, use of high carbon ferrochromes has fallen and chrome ores with lower chrome and chrome-iron ratios have been more widely used. South Africa and the USSR dominate the supply side and the main consuming countries are not producers. Chromium could be recycled from scrap but less than 10 per cent is now recycled. There is an active free market.

Cobalt

Owing to the disruption of supplies from the main producer, Zaire, in the late 1970s and the consequent high price of cobalt, there has been a major shift towards substituting and reducing the cobalt content of alloys. Cobalt remains an important component of almost all permanent magnet materials and cobalt-based superalloys are important components in jet engines and gas turbines. There is no effective substitute for its metallurgical applications although in this area and in a number of other areas of present use, considerable research effort is being devoted to finding suitable replacements. Deep sea manganese nodules are a potential source of supply for cobalt.

Columbium (Niobium)

Columbium is usually produced as a by-product or co-product from tin mining, or with tantalum. Brazil and Canada supply over 95 per cent of the world's columbium production and this dependence means that supplies would be vulnerable to almost any form of production restriction. Recycling is insignificant and possible substitutes would have to be used in greater quantity than columbium especially in its stainless and HSLA steel uses.

Germanium

At present, germanium production comes entirely as a minor by-product of zinc ores, but there is a potentially large source of recycling from high-purity optical devices and there is a large supply of germanium recoverable from the ash and flue dusts from the combustion of coal in power generation. The market for germanium is very small and prices can be quickly responsive to variations in demand or supply. It is difficult to find suitable substitutes with the same reliability as germanium.

Hafnium

Hanium is recovered as a by-product of the production of hafnium-free nuclear-grade zirconium base alloys. It has no substitute for its uses in nuclear reactor control rods and refractory metal alloys. The demand for zirconium is the necessary prerequisite for hafnium production.

Indium

Indium is a minor by-product of lead and zinc smelting and refining. It has substitutes in many of its uses but its cost advantage favours its continued use. Its dependence on lead and zinc processing is the only limit to its supply and indium is used in industries that may grow at a faster rate than those using zinc.

Lithium

Lithium is produced as the major product from pegmatite ores and from brine. Aluminium potlines, glass, ceramics and lubrication have been lithium's main uses but its greatest potential lies in its use in lithium batteries. There are ample production sources and several new sources.

Manganese

Its indispensability in the steelmaking process has placed it on the vital list for most industrialised economies. The USSR and South Africa dominate world production but in the long-run manganese nodules from the ocean floor offer an unlimited supply. Present prices are too low to make this potential source economic or to justify recovery through recycling. There is a producer price but also a free market.

Mercury

Cinnabar deposits mined for their mercury content are the primary source of production. Environmental considerations have limited the uses of mercury but for those remaining the only possible substitutes are more expensive. Since the failure of the mercury producers to establish a cartel, sales have been largely at free market prices.

Molybdenum

The USA is self-sufficient in molybdenum and Canada has several existing producers and a number of new sources. Molybdenum, which is derived from porphyry molybdenum, copper-molybdenum deposits or as a copper by-product, has a wide range of uses including nuclear and aerospace hardware. Oversupply rather than shortages is its main problem.

Nickel

Mainly derived from nickel-copper or iron sulphides, nickel is mostly produced in Canada and the USSR but there are a number of other producers. Over 90 per cent of its use is in alloys with other metals and its use is favoured there due to its low cost and good performance. Nickel is traded at producer prices, in a free market and in a futures market. There is no present shortage of supply.

Platinum Group Metals

Platinum is mined as a primary mineral only in South Africa and is produced as a by-product of palladium in the USSR and as a by-product of nickel mining in Canada. South Africa and the USSR dominate production of all the platinum group metals. These metals are all relatively high cost which has concentrated their applications where there are no satisfactory substitutes. Users of these metals normally hold large stocks and these could provide a year's leeway before a supply disruption became critical.

Rhenium

Rhenium is derived from molybdenite which is itself obtained from porphyry copper or copper-molybdenum deposits. Over 90 per cent of its use is in catalysts in low-lead and lead-free gasoline but it has the potential for much wider use in areas where its high density, high modulus of elasticity and high melting point could be used to advantage.

Selenium

A by-product of the copper refining process, selenium is produced in Japan, Canada, the United States and other countries. Plain paper copiers and glass manufacture are its major uses. About 15 per cent of production can be recycled annually. The main selenium product, high purity selenium, is not traded on the free market but the range of possible substitutes probably puts a constraint on the possible price.

Tantalum

Tantalite is mostly produced as a by-product of tin mining, tin slags or as a co-product with columbite. Its major uses are in capacitors for military applications and in communications, data processing and consumer electronics. Canada, Brazil and Australia are the main producers, although the USSR appears to have the world's largest deposits. Tantalum's uses as a carbide and in the aerospace industry as a metal have seriously declined and while still important, demand is now less than available supply. There is a free market for tantalum but it appears that less than 10 per cent of annual production is traded there.

Tellurium

Tellurium is a by-product of copper and lead refining and has also been identified in the composition of deep-sea manganese nodules. Most of the known tellurium deposits are in North America. Tellurium has substitutes in its major uses.

Titanium

Titanium is derived from beach sand deposits that contain ilmenite and rutile. Its major use is as a metal or alloy in jet engines, airframes, space and missile applications, for most of which it has no effective substitute. South Africa and Australia have major reserves and there is oversupply at present. Environmental restrictions appear to pose the only possible threat to supply.

Tungsten

Tungsten is the primary product obtained from wolfram and scheelite. Its major uses are in tool steels and in cutting and wear-resistant materials. The USSR and China are major producers but Canada and the United States are producers and have reserves. Recycling could also increase potential supply.

Vanadium

Usually recovered as a co-product with uranium, iron or phosphorus, vanadium has its major use in HSLA steels. South Africa, the USSR and China are the major producers, with around 40 per cent coming from South Africa. The possible substitutes for vanadium are mostly more expensive but molybdenum is a sufficiently close substitute to be used without major problems if the supply of vanadium was restricted. Australia is expected to become an important producer in the 1980s, but is still only a potential supplier. Most vanadium is sold at producer prices although there is a free market.

Zirconium

Zirconium is obtained from the mineral zircon which is mined from beach sands. Its main uses are in refractories and foundries. Australia, South Africa and the USA are major producers and have considerable reserves. There has been an unsuccessful attempt to establish a zirconium cartel that led to the growth of a free market in zirconium.

Prospects for Strategic Materials

Of the strategic materials considered here, beryllium, chromium and columbium are the three in which a critical supply situation could arise most easily. There are restricted sources of supply for each of these materials. A second group is characterised by the existence of potential new sources of supply that would remove most of the risk of disruption but these sources are not being developed at present prices. This group, comprising germanium, cobalt, manganese, platinum group metals and vanadium, includes many of those listed as critical for industrialised nations.

In present circumstances the remaining strategic materials appear either to be in inadequate supply or to have close substitutes that could make up any shortfall.

While there may be grounds for stockpiling beryllium, chromium and columbium, for the materials in the second group a more appropriate strategy would be to sponsor the development of the potential new sources instead of stockpiling. This would ensure continued availability of the materials.

Beryllium, germanium, selenium and tantalum have small markets which could be subject to manipulation in the short-run, and the possibility of increased holdings of these materials in government and private sector stockpiles could make these markets even narrower and more easily-manipulated. This danger appears to have at least as high a probability as supply disruption.

APPENDIX I: STOCKPILING OF STRATEGIC MATERIALS IN THE UNITED STATES

The History and Operation of Stockpiling in the USA

Simon Strauss points out (1978) that during the Second World War, 'strategic' materials were those that were basically imported, while 'critical' materials were those materials that were essential to the war effort but able to be produced in the USA. Measures were taken during the Second World War to ensure sufficient availability of materials for the war effort and at the war's end the government held quantities of almost all strategic and critical materials.

In 1946 Congress introduced the *Strategic and Critical Materials Stock Piling Act* (50 USC) which has provided the basis for all of the stockpile activity since that time. In order to counter the concern of the mining industry that the government, having acquired large quantities of these materials, might dispose of them at some future date with ruinous consequences for the markets of those materials, the Act provided that disposals from the stockpile required the advice and consent of Congress.

During the Korean War some spot shortages of materials occurred and legislation was enacted empowering the Administration to enter into contracts with producers to encourage them to create new productive capacity for the purpose of selling the material produced to industry, but if there was no market for the material, it could be delivered to the stockpile. Although these provisions were intended for domestic producers they were available also to producers outside the United States. At this time the quantities held in the stockpile were classified but when President Kennedy took office he issued a statement saying that, having examined the stockpile accumulations, he believed they were excessive and proposed that the objectives should be reviewed, and that Congress should investigate the stockpile situation. Senator Symington carried out the suggested investigation over a period of two and a half years.

It became clear from that investigation that although the goals for individual materials had originally been established under the control of the Army-Navy Munitions Board and later the Federal Preparedness Agency (and its predecessors), the Departments of the Interior,

Commerce, Agriculture, Treasury and State and the Council of Economic Advisors were also involved.

In determining the stockpile objectives, the criteria used included the time-span of a probable conflict, the likely allies and enemies, the reliability of sources, the extent of the military requirements and whether the war would be nuclear or not; but these criteria would be accorded different weights at different times so that no clear pattern of objectives was discernible.

A programme of selling from the stockpile was initiated in 1963 and was undertaken by the General Services Administration. Under the successive Presidencies of Johnson and Nixon the stockpile was used for price controls.

In 1973 President Nixon attempted to redefine the stockpile policy, instituting the standard that only the materials necessary for a one-year war ought to be stockpiled on the assumption that any future war would only be of one year's duration and if it extended beyond that time new mines could be opened or substitute materials used. The implementation of this new objective would have led to a reduction in the value of the stockpile from over $US eight billion to less than $US one billion.

Both Congress and the Subcommittee of the House Armed Services Committee (the latter passes on stockpile disposal bills) were not prepared to adopt the Nixon proposals and only some half a million dollars worth of materials were sold in late 1973 and early 1974. Copper, tin and aluminium were the main materials sold. The Chairman of the House Subcommittee, Congressman Bennett, succeeded in encouraging the new Ford Administration to take a further look at stockpile goals. As a result of that review new goals were set based on the premise of a three-year rather than a one-year war and these varied widely from earlier estimates for many materials. The Carter Administration included stockpile replenishment funds in its budget requests in 1979 and 1980 but Congress refused to appropriate the necessary funds.

In September 1980 the American Geological Institute, which represents 18 professional geological associations with 50,000 members, warned the major US Presidential candidates that the USSR was trying to halt or interrupt US access to minerals critical to national defence at a time when US stockpiles of 93 strategic materials were as much as 80 per cent short of their goals. Grover E.Murray, President of the Institute, said in the Institute's statement that:

Without manganese, chromium, platinum and cobalt, there can be no automobiles, no airplanes, no jet engines, no satellites and no sophisticated weapons – not even home appliances.

The Institute was expressing a concern already written about in *Fortune* and *Business Week* which had also noted the policy shift by the USSR, for long an important exporter of many materials, to reduce its exports considerably and to enter the market as an importer of a number of strategic materials, developments which might be the preliminaries to increasing competition for the world supplies of strategic materials.

Table A1:1: US National Defence Stockpile Inventory of Strategic and Critical Materials as at September 1980

	Commodity Group	Unit	1980 Goal	Inventory	$US Million Value of Inventory	Quantity after Crediting Offset Excess	Deficit
1.	Aluminium Metal Group	ST A1 metal	7,150,000	3,444,064	551.1		3,705,936
2.	Aluminium Oxide/ Abrasive Grain group	ST Ab grain	638,000	259,124	124.0		378,876
3.	Antimony	ST	36,000	40,730	163.7	4,730	
4.	Asbestos, Amosite	ST	17,000	42,534	21.9	25,534	
5.	Asbestos, Chrysotile	ST	3,000	9,958	8.9	6,958	
6.	Bauxite, Refractory	LCT	1,400,000	174,599	34.0		1,225,401
7.	Beryllium Metal Group	ST	1,220	1,061	150.1		159
8.	Bismuth	LB	2,200,000	2,081,298	5.2		118,702
9.	Cadmium	LB	11,700,000	6,328,729	15.8		5,371,271
10.	Castor Oil (Sebacic Acid)	LB	22,000,000	5,009,697	8.9		9,475,757
11.	Chromium, Chemical and Metallurgical Group	ST Cr metal	1,353,000	1,173,230	1,033.8		179,770
12.	Chromite, Refractory Grade Ore	SDT	850,000	391,414	36.9		458,586
13.	Cobalt	LB Co	85,400,000	40,802,393	1,020.1		44,597,607
14.	Columbium Group	LB Cb metal	4,850,000	2,310,528	37.7		2,339,472
15.	Copper	ST	1,000,000	29,048	65.1		970,952
16.	Cordage Fibres, Abaca	LB	155,000,000	nil	–		155,000,000
17.	Cordage Fibres, Sisal	LB	60,000,000	nil	–		60,000,000
18.	Diamond, Industrial Group	KT	29,700,000	42,929,316	416.1	13,229,316	
19.	Feathers and Down	LB	1,500,000	nil	–		1,500,000
20.	Fluorspar, Acid Grade	SDT	1,400,000	895,983	125.4		504,017
21.	Fluorspar, Metallurgical Grade	SDT	1,700,000	411,738	40.1		1,288,262
22.	Graphite, Natural, Ceylon, Amorphous Lump	ST	6,300	5,498	5.2		802
23.	Graphite, Natural, Malagasy, Crystalline	ST	20,000	17,911	11.9		2,089

24.	Graphite, Natural, Other than Ceylon and Malagasy	ST	2,800	2,802	0.5	2	
25.	Iodine	LB	5,800,000	8,013,074	47.3	2,213,074	
26.	Jewel Bearings	PC	120,000,000	68,731,890	61.2		51,268,110
27.	Lead	ST	1,100,000	601,036	504.9		498,964
28.	Manganese, Dioxide, Battery Grade Group	SDT	87,000	250,643	23.3	163,643	
29.	Manganese, Chemical and Metallurgical Group	ST Mn metal	1,500,000	1,586,581	529.8	86,581	
30.	Mercury	FL	10,500	191,391	78.0	180,891	
31.	Mica Muscovite Block, Stained and Better	LB	6,200,000	5,212,444	27.8		987,556
32.	Mica Muscovite Film, First and Second Qualities	LB	90,000	1,274,493	14.9	1,184,495	
33.	Mica Muscovite Splittings	LB	12,630,000	19,546,395	39.1	6,916,395	
34.	Mica Phlogopite Block	LB	210,000	130,745	0.1		79,255
35.	Mica Phlogopite Splittings	LB	930,000	2,019,537	2.0	1,089,537	
36.	Molybdenum Group	LB Mo	nil	nil			
37.	Nickel	ST Ni Co	20,000	nil			200,000
38.	Opium Group	AMA LB	130,000	71,303	29.6		58,697
39.	Platinum Group Metals, Iridium	Tr Oz	98,000	16,991	10.2		81,009
40.	Platinum Group Metals Palladium	Tr Oz	3,000,000	1,255,003	282.4		1,744,997
41.	Platinum Group Metals, Platinum	Tr Oz	1,310,000	452,640	215.0		857,360
42.	Pyrethrum	LB	500,000	nil			500,000
43.	Quartz Crystals	LB	600,000	2,423,036	14.5	1,823,036	
44.	Quinidine	Av Oz	10,100,000	1,800,462	7.8		8,299,538
45.	Rubber	LT	850,000	119,208	172.2		730,792
46.	Rutile	SDT	106,000	39,186	12.7		66,814
47.	Sapphire and Ruby	KT	nil	16,305,502	.2	16,305,502	

Table A1: 1 US National Defence Stockpile Inventory of Strategic and Critical Materials as at September 1980 (Continued)

	Commodity	Unit	1980 Goal	Inventory	$US Million Value of Inventory	Quantity after Crediting Offset Excess	Deficit
48.	Silicon Carbide, Crude	ST	29,000	80,550	36.2	51,550	
49.	Silver, Fine	Tr Oz	nil	139,500,000	1,848.4	139,500,000	
50.	Talc, Steatite Block and Lump	ST	28	1,092	4	1,064	
51.	Tantalum Group	LB Ta metal	7,160,000	2,391,940	343.9		4,768,060
	Taltalum, Carbide Powder	LB Ta	nil	28,688	5.0		
	Tantalum Metal	LB Ta	nil	201,133	28.2		
	Tantalum Minerals	LB Ta	8,400,000	2,551,302	310.7		h
52.	Thorium Nitrate	LB	600,000	7,141,812	19.6	6,541,812	
53.	Tin	LT	42,000	200,112	2,900.6	158,112	
54.	Titanium Sponge	ST	195,000	32,331	440.3		162,669
55.	Tungsten Group	LB W metal	50,666,000	80,814,761	861.8	30,148,761	
	Tungsten Carbide Powder	LB W	2,000,000	2,032,942	30.2		
	Tungsten, Ferro	LB W	nil	2,025,361	24.1		
	Tungsten, Metal Powder	LB W	1,600,000	1,898,911	26.4		
	Tungsten Ores and Concentrates	LB W	55,540,000	87,964,215	781.1		
56.	Vanadium Group	ST V Metal	8,700	541	5.9		8,159
	Vanadium, Ferro	ST V	1,000	nil	–		1,000
	Vanadium Pentoxide	ST V	7,700	541	5.9		7,159
57	Vegetable Tannin Extract, Chestnut	LT	5,000	16,717	9.0	11,717	
58.	Vegetable Tannin Extract, Quebracho	LT	28,000	142,691	84.2	114,691	
59.	Vegetable Tannin Extract, Wattle	LT	15,000	16,398	9.2	1,398	
60.	Zinc	ST	1,425,000	375,970	320.5		1,049,030

Notes:

AMA LB = anhydrous morphine alkaloid (lb)
Av Oz = avoirdupois oz
FL = flask (76-lb)
KT = carat
LB = lb
LB Cb = lb of contained columbium
LB Co = lb of contained cobalt
LB Mo = lb of contained molybdenum
LB Ta = lb of contained tantalum
LB W = lb of contained tungsten
LCT = long calcined ton
LT = long ton
PC = piece
SDT = short dry ton
ST = short ton
ST Ni+Co = short tons of contained nickel plus cobalt
ST V = short tons of contained vanadium
Tr Oz = troy oz

APPENDIX 2: OPERATING MINES IN THE WESTERN WORLD YIELDING STRATEGIC MATERIALS AS AT JANUARY 1983

	Mine	*Location*	*Materials Produced*
North America	*Canada*		
	Brenda	British Columbia	Cu, Mo
	Copper Mountain	Quebec	Cu, Mo
	Highmont	British Columbia	Cu, Mo
	Island Copper	British Columbia	Cu, Mo
	Jersey	British Columbia	Cu, Mo
	Lornex	British Columbia	Cu, Mo
	McLeese Lake	British Columbia	Cu, Mo
	Needle Mountain	Quebec	Cu, Mo
	Thierry	Ontario	Cu, Ni
	Chisel Lake	Manitoba	Zn, Ag, Cu, Pb, Cd
	Coleman	Ontario	Ni, Cu
	Copper Cliff South	Ontario	Ni, Cu
	Creighton	Ontario	Ni, Cu
	East	Ontario	Ni, Cu
	Falconbridge	Ontario	Ni, Cu
	Fraser	Ontario	Ni, Cu
	Frood	Ontario	Ni, Cu
	Garson	Ontario	Ni, Cu
	Levack	Ontario	Ni, Cu
	Little Stobie	Ontario	Ni, Cu
	Lockerly	Ontario	Ni, Cu
	McCreedy West	Ontario	Ni, Cu
	North	Ontario	Ni, Cu
	Onaping	Ontario	Ni, Cu
	Pipe	Manitoba	Ni, Cu
	Shebandowan	Ontario	Ni, Cu
	Stobie	Ontario	Ni, Cu
	Strathcona	Ontario	Ni, Cu
	Thompson	Manitoba	Ni, Cu
	Havre St Pierre	Quebec	Fe, Ti
	Barker Creek	Yukon	Au, Pt
	Dublin Gulch	Yukon	Au, W
	Boss Mountain	British Columbia	Mo
	Endako	British Columbia	Mo
	Kitsault	British Columbia	Mo
	Canada Tungsten	Northwest Territories	W
	St Honoré	Quebec	Cb
	Bernic Lake	Manitoba	Ta, Cs
	United States		
	Coeur	Idaho	Ag, Cu, Sb
	Bagdad	Arizona	Cu, Mo

	Berkeley	Montana	Cu, Ag, Mo
	Bingham Canyon	Utah	Cu, Mo, Au, Ag, Re
	Chino	New Mexico	Cu, Ag, Mo
	Copper Flats	New Mexico	Cu, Mo, Au, Ag
	Esperanza	Arizona	Cu, Mo
	Inspiration	Arizona	Cu, Mo
	Mineral Park	Arizona	Cu, Mo
	Mission	Arizona	Cu, Mo, Ag
	Pima	Arizona	Cu, Mo, Ag
	Pinto Valley	Arizona	Cu, Mo
	Ray	Arizona	Cu, Ag, Mo
	San Manuel	Arizona	Cu, Mo, Au, Ag, Re
	Sierrita	Arizona	Cu, Mo, Ag, Re
	Twin Buttes	Arizona	Cu, Ag, Mo
	Sterling	New Jersey	Zn, Fe, Mn
	Climax	Colorado	Mo, W
	Henderson	Colorado	Mo
	Questa	New Mexico	Mo
	Tonopah	Nevada	Mo
	Ambrosia Lake	New Mexico	U, Mo
	Canon City/Schwartzwalder	Colorado	U, Mo
	Uravan	Colorado	U, V
	McDermitt	Nevada	Hg
	Boulogne	Florida	Ti, Zr, Monazite
	Green Cove Springs	Florida	Ti, Zr, Monazite
	Highland	Florida	Ti
	Manchester	New Jersey	Ti
	Trail Ridge	Florida	Ti, Zr
	Emerson	Nevada	W
	Pine Creek	California	W, Mo
	Springer	Nevada	W
	Nickel Mountain	Oregon	Ni
	MacIntyre	New York	Ti
Central and South America	***Bolivia***		
	Caracoles	La Paz	Sn, Bi, W
	Cerro de Potosi	Potosi	Sn, Ag, W
	Chojilla	Yungas	Sn, W
	Colquiri	Colquiri	Sn, W
	Quechisla	Potosi	Sn, Bi, W
	San Jose	Oruro	Sn, Pb, Ag, Sb
	Enramada	Yungas	W
	Kami	Potosi	W
	Tazna	Potosi	W
	Brazil		
	Santana	Matto Grosso	Mn
	Serro do Navio	Amapa	Mn
	Urucum	Matto Grosso	Mn
	Pratopolis	Minas Gerais	Ni
	Niquelandia (Codemin)	Minas Gerais	Ni
	Niquelandia (Tocantins)	Minas Gerais	Ni
	Campo Formosa	Bahia	Cr
	Brasimet	Guias	Nb

	CBMM	Minas Gerais	Nb
	Volta Grande	Minas Gerais	Sn, Ta
	Barra Verde	Pernambuco	W
	Brejui	Rio Grande do Norte	W
	Chile		
	Andina	Aconcagua	Cu, Mo
	Chinquicamata	El hoa	Cu, Mo
	El Salvador	Atacama	Cu, Mo, Ag, Au
	El Teniente	O'Higgins	Cu, Mo
	Colombia		
	Cerro Matoso	Cordoba	Ni
	Cuba		
	Mayari	Oriente	Ni, Co
	Moa Bay	Oriente	Ni, Co
	Nicaro	Oriente	Ni, Co
	Dominican Republic		
	Falcondo	Bonao	Ni
	Mexico		
	Inquaran	Michoacan	Cu, Ag, W
	Tecolote	Sonora	Cu, W, Zn, Ag
	Molango	Hidalgo	Mn
	Cumobabi	Sonora	Mo, Cu
	Peru		
	Casapalca	Casapalca	Ag, Zn, Ph , Au, W, Cu
	Julcani	Huancavelica	Ag, W
	Aquila	Cerro de Pasco	Cu, Mo
	Cuajone	Moquegua	Cu, Mo, Ag
	Monterrosas	Ica	Cu, Au, Ag, Mo
	Toquepala	Moquegua	Cu, Mo, Ag
Australasia	*Australia*		
	Agnew	Western Australia	Ni
	Greenvale	Queensland	Ni, Co
	Kambalda	Western Australia	Ni, Cu
	Windarra	Western Australia	Ni, Cu
	Rossarden	Tasmania	Sn, W
	King Island	Tasmania	W
	Wolfram Camp	Queensland	W, Mo
	Greenbushes	Western Australia	Sn, Ta, Cb
	Moolyella	Western Australia	Sn, Ta
	Allied Eneabba	Western Australia	Ti, Zr, Monazite
	Capel (AMC)	Western Australia	Ti, Zr
	Capel (Cable Sands)	Western Australia	Ti, Zr, Monazite
	Crescent Head	New South Wales	Ti, Zr, Monazite
	Eneabba	Western Australia	Ti, Zr
	Harrington	New South Wales	Ti, Zr, Monazite

	Hawks Nest	New South Wales	Ti, Zr, Monazite
	Jerusalem Creek	New South Wales	Ti, Zr, Monazite
	Jurien Bay	Western Australia	Ti, Zr
	Moreton Bay	Queensland	Ti, Zr, Monazite
	North Capel	Western Australia	Ti, Zr, Monazite
	North Stradbroke (AMC)	Queensland	Ti, Zr, Monazite
	North Stradbroke (CRC)	Queensland	Ti, Zr, Monazite
	Tomago	New South Wales	Ti, Zr, Monazite
	Yoganup	Western Australia	Ti, Zr, Monazite
	Mt Carbine	Queensland	W
	Torrington	New South Wales	W
	Groote Eylandt	Northern Territory	Mn
	Wundowie	Western Australia	V
	New Caledonia		
	CGMC		Ni
	Group Pentecost		Ni
	Montagnat Mines		Ni
	Kouaoua		Ni
	Nepoui		Ni
	Poro		Ni
	Thio		Ni
	Tiebaghi		Cr
	Vanuatu		
	Forari		Mn
Europe	*Austria*		
	Bleiberg	Carinthia	Zr, Pb, Sb
	Mittersill	Salzburg	W
	Finland		
	Keretti	Outokumpu	Zu, Zn, Co
	Luikonlahti	Kaavi	Cu, Zn, Co, Pyrite
	Vuonos	Outokumpu	Cu, Zr, Co, Ni
	Hitura	Nivala	Ni
	Kotalahti	Leppavirta	Ni, Cu
	Vammala	Vammala	Ni
	Kemi	Kemi	Cr
	Otanmaki	Vuolijoki	Fe, Ti, V
	Mustavaara	Taivalkoski	Fe, V
	France		
	Salau	Ariege	W
	Greece		
	Larymna	Euboea	Ni, Co
	Norway		
	Raudsand	Raudsand	Fe, V, Ti
	Titania	Haugei Dalane	Ti, Fe,Ni, Pyrite
	Portugal		
	Beralt	Beira Baixa	W, Sn, Cu

	Burralha	Tras-os-Montes	W
	Spain		
	Barruecopardo	Salamanca	W, As
	Almaden	Almaden	Hg
	Sweden		
	Yxsjöberg	Horken	W, Cu
Africa	*Botswana*		
	Pikwe	Pikwe	Cu, Ni
	Gabon		
	Ogooué	Moanda	Mn
	Ghana		
	Nsuta	Wassaw	Mn
	Malagasy		
	Kraomita Malagasy	Andriamena	Cr
	Morocco		
	Bou Azzer	Ouarzazate	Co, Ni
	Imini	Trans Atlas	Mn
	Rwanda		
	Somirwa	Kigali	Sn, W
	South Africa		
	Palabora	Transvaal	Cu, Fe, U, Zr, Ag
	Mapuchs	Transvaal	Fe, V
	Hotazel	Cape Province	Mn
	Lohathla	Cape Province	Mn
	Mamatwan	Cape Province	Mn
	Mancorp Mines	Cape Province	Mn
	Middleplaats	Cape Province	Mn
	Wessels	Cape Province	Mn
	Kilokong	Transvaal	Cr
	Grasvally	Transvaal	Cr
	Grootbroom	Transvaal	Cr
	Grouthoek	Transvaal	Cr
	Hendriksplaats	Transvaal	Cr
	Henry Gould	Transvaal	Cr
	Jagdlust	Transvaal	Cr
	Millsell	Transvaal	Cr
	Mooinooi	Transvaal	Cr
	Nthuane	Bophuthatswana	Cr
	Ruighuek	Bophuthatswana	Cr
	Strydfontein	Bophuthatswana	Cr
	Winterveld	Transvaal	Cr
	Szartkop	Transvaal	Cr
	Amandelbult	Transvaal	Pt, Ni, Cu
	Atok	Transvaal	Pt, Ni
	Bafokeng North	Bophuthatswana	Pt, Ni, Cu
	Bafokeng South	Bophuthatswana	Pt, Ni, Cu

	Rustenburg	Bophuthatswana	Pt, Ni, Cu
	Union	Bophuthatswana	Pt, Ni
	Western Platinum	Transvaal	Pt, Ni
	Wildebeestfontein North	Bophuthatswana	Pt, Ni, Cu
	Consolidated Murchison	Transvaal	Sb
	Brits (Ucar)	Bophuthatswana	V
	Richards Bay	Natal	Ti, Zr, Fe
	Namibia (SW Africa)		
	Berg Aukas	Grootfontein	Zn, Pb, V
	Brandberg West	Brandberg	Sn, W
	Sudan		
	Ingessana Hills	Ingessana	Cr
	Nile Mining	Ingessana	Cr
	Zaire		
	Di Kuluwe-Mashamba	Shaba	Cu, Co
	Kakanda	Shaba	Cu, Co
	Kambore	Shaba	Cu, Co
	Kamoto	Shaba	Cu, Co
	Mupine-Musonoi	Shaba	Cu, Co
	Mutoshi	Shaba	Cu, Co
	Kisenge	Kisenge	Mn
	Symetain	Kalima	Sn, Nb, Ta
	Zairetain	Manono	Sn, Ta, Nb
	Zambia		
	Baluba	Luanshya	Cu, Co
	Chambishi	Kalulushi	Cu, Co
	Chibuluma	Kalulushi	Cu, Co
	Nkana-Mindola	Kitwe	Cu, Co
	Zimbabwe		
	Empress	Gatooma	Ni, Cu
	Epoch	Filabusi	Ni
	Madziwa	Bindura	Ni, Cu
	Trojan	Bindura	Ni, Cu
	Shangani	Inyati	Ni
	Selukwe Peak	Selukwe	Cr
Asia	*India*		
	Chavara	Kerala	Ti, Zr
	Balapur	Maharashta	Mn
	Bhutuda	Orissa	Mn
	Dalapahar	Orissa	Mn
	Gurda	Orissa	Mn
	Siljora	Orissa	Mn
	Thakurani	Orissa	Mn
	Jadugada	Bihar	U, Cu, Mo
	Indonesia		
	Gebe	Maluccas	Ni
	Pomalaa	Sulawesi	Ni

Soroako	Sulawesi	Ni
Iran		
Shahriah	Fariah	Cr
Japan		
Kamaishi	Iwate	Fe, Cu, W
Korea (Republic)		
Sangdong	Kangwon-do	W, Mo
Malaysia		
Austral Amalgamated	Perak	Sn, Ti
Bidor	Perak	Sn, Ti, Zr, Au, Monazite
Etains de Kinta	Perak	Sn, Ti
Tasek Chini	Pahang	Mn
Bau	Sarawak	Sb
Philippines		
Masinloc	Zambales	Cr
Palawan Quicksilver	Palawan	Hg
Nonoc	Nonoc Is	Ni
Rio Tuba	Palawan	Ni
Basay	Negros Occidental	Cu, Au, Ag, Mo
Lutopan	Cebu	Cu, Au, Ag, Mo
Sipalay	Negros Occidental	Cu, Au, Ag, Mo
Sri Lanka		
Pulmoddai	Pulmoddai	Ti, Zr
Thailand		
Samoeng	Chingmai	W, Sn
Turkey		
Cinkur Mines	Konya-Elazig	Zr, Pb, Cd, Ag
Guleman	Elazig	Cr
Karak	Siras	Cr
Uc Kopru	Mugla	Cr
Uludag	Bursa Uludag	W
Halikoy	Izmir	Hg
Konya	Konya	Hg
Ozdemir	Tokat	Sb

Notes:

Ag	Silver	Cd	Cadmium
As	Arsenic	Co	Cobalt
Au	Gold	Cr	Chromium
Bi	Bismuth	Cs	Caesium
Cb	Colombium	Cu	Copper

Fe	Iron	Sn	Tin
Hg	Mercury	Ta	Tantalum
Mn	Manganese	Ti	Titanium
Mo	Molybdenum	U	Uranium
Ni	Nickel	V	Vanadium
Pb	Lead	W	Tungsten
Pt	Platinum	Zn	Zinc
Re	Rhenium	Zr	Zirconium
Sb	Antimony		

APPENDIX 3: MAJOR NEW PROJECTS AND EXPANSION PROGRAMMES KNOWN AT JANUARY 1983

	Company	Location	Materials	Details
North America	*Canada*			
	Bethlehem Copper/ Valley Copper	Highland Valley, BC	Cu, Mo	20,000 tonnes a day production
	Liard Copper	Schaft Creek, BC	Cu, Mo	Evaluating reserves
	Placer/Adanac Mining	Atlin, BC	Mo	Ruby Creek – 15,000 tonnes a day operation
	Inco Metals	Thompson, Manitoba	Ni	Deferred until 1986
	Inco Metals	Port Colborne, Ontario	Co metal	New electrolytic plant, 1983
	Amax Exploration	Mactung, NW Territories	W	
	Brunswick Tin/ Billiton	Charlotte County, New Brunswick	W, Mo	650,000 tonnes a year operation. Behind schedule, 1983
	Highwood Resources	Thor Lake, NW Territories	Ta, Nb	Evaluating reserves
	United States			
	Anaconda	Stillwater, Montana	Pt, Pd	New mine and plant planned
	Manville Corp./ Chevron	Stillwater, Montana	Pt, Pd	700,000 tonnes a year operation development decision due in 1983
	Anschutz Corp.	Fredricktown, Missouri	Co	Seeking government assistance to re-open Madison mine
	Noranda	Blackbird, Idaho	Co, Cu	Startup of 1,800 tonnes a year operation depends on government contracts
	California Nickel/ Cook International	Gasquet Mt, California	Ni, Co, Cr concentrates	Feasibility studies for 9,000 tonnes/ yr Ni, 908 tonnes/ yr Co and 45,000/ Cr concentrates
	US Antimony Corp	Thompson Falls, Montana	Sb	Doubling plant capacity to 550

				tonnes a day
	Amax	Mt Emmons, Colorado	Mo	Feasibility studies of Crested Butte project
	Amoco (Cyrus)	Thompson Creek, Idaoho	Mo	Development under way of 9,000 tonnes a year Mo in concentrates project
	Molycorp	Questa, New Mexico	Mo	New 60,000 tonnes a day mine development
	US Borax	Quartz Hill, Alaska	Mo	60,000 tonnes a day operation development decision due 1984
	Union Carbide/ Hecla	Moab, Utah	U, V	Development of Lisbon Valley mine, 250 tonnes a day
	Westinghouse/ Mitsubishi	Ogden, Utah	Ti metal, Zr	Feasibility study under way
Central and South America	*Argentina*			
	Cia Minera Aguila	El Pachon, San Juan	Cu, Mo, Cu metal	Evaluation complete but development uncertain
	Bolivia			
	Churquiuni Enterprises	Chicote Grande	W	180,000 tonnes a year new mine being developed
	Brazil			
	CVRD	Igarape Azul, Para	Mn	500,000 tonnes a year operation, expected to replace Serro de Navio
	Metais de Goias	Anicuns, Gorias	Ni metal	New plant producing 2,000 tonnes a year Ni metal due for completion during 1983
	Rutilo e Ilmenita do Brasil	Mataroca, Pernambuco	Ilmenite concentrates, Zr	New development to produce 100,000 tonnes a year of ilmenite concentrates and 15,000 tonnes a year Zr
	Metais de Goias	Ouvidor, Goias	Nb_2O_5	Feasibility of mining 10 million

				tonnes containing 1.06% Nb_2O_5 being considered
	Chile			
	Codelco	Salar de Pedernales Salar de Atacama	Lithium, boron Li	Feasibility studies for 1.3 million tonne Li plant being developed
	Ecominas	Pantanos-Pegardorcito, Antioquia	Cu, Mo	Pre-feasibility studies
	Cuba			
	Cubaniquel	Punta Gorda	Ni metal	Plant due for completion in 1985
	Ecuador			
	DGGM (government)	Chuca, Loja	Cu, Mo	Evaluating reserves
	Mexico			
	Cia Fresnillo	Fresnillo, Zacatecas	Ag, W, Mo	Mine and mill expansion pending approval
	Cia Minera Autlan	Molenago, Hidalgo	Mn	680,000 tonnes a year operation under development
	Peru			
	Centromin	Toromocho	Cu, Zn, Mo, Ag	Feasibility studies for a 30,000 tonnes a day operation under way
	Mineroperu	Antamina, Ancash	Cu, Zn, Mo, Ag	Looking for partner to develop 10,000 tonne a day operation
	Soc. Minera Rio Seco	Pisco	Cu, Co	Finance sought for mine development
	Centromin	Atapaca, Tacna	Pb, Zn, Cu, Ag, Mo	Pilot testing of complex ore reserves
Australasia	*Australia*			
	Gemco	Groote Eylandt, Northern Territory	Mn	Planning mine expansion of 6 million tonnes a year for 1990
	Metals Ex/	Widgiemooltha,	Ni	Feasibility studies

	Outopkumpu	Western Australia		under way
	Pacific Copper	Jingellic, New South Wales	Sn, W	Development considered
	Petrocarb/Peko Wallsend	Molyhill, Northern Territory	W, Mo	Reserves being evaluated to increase production
	Tasminex-McIntyre	Burnie, Tasmania	W	Evaluation under way
	Union Carbide/ Minefields	Mt Mulgine, Western Australia	W	Evaluation of possible 10,000 tonnes a day operation
	Greenbushes Tin	Greenbushes, Western Australia	Ta, Sn, Li	Planned 250,000 tonnes a year development
	CSR	Mt Pleasant, New South Wales	Mo	Under evaluation
	Minatome	Townsville, Queensland	U, Mo	Australian partners sought for 350 tonnes a year Ben Lomond development
	Yeelirrie Development	Yeelirrie, Western Australia	U, V	Planned development for 1985-6
	New Zealand			
	NZ Nickel Smelters	—	Fe, Ni	Plans for 40,000 tonne a year smelter fed by ore from New Caledonia
	Papua New Guinea			
	Nord Highland	Madang	Cr_2O_3, Ni, Co	Ramu River deposits being evaluated
Europe	*Finland*			
	Outokumpu Oy	Econkoski	Ni, Cu	500,000 tonnes a year mine development under consideration
	France			
	Penarroya	Montredon, Tarn	W	Feasibility studies
	Penarroya	Allier	Sn, Ta	Feasibility studies
	Greece			
	Hellenic Ferroalloys	Tsigheti, Almyros	Fe, Cr	30,000 tonnes a year project coming into operation
	Hellenic Ferroalloys	Mt Vourino, Kozani	Cr	250,000 tonnes a year develop-

				ment with 60,000 tonne Cr concentrate dressing plant
	UK			
	SW Consolidated Resources	Collington Cornwall	Sn, W	Reopening Redmoor/Prince of Wales properties
	Amax/Billiton	Hemerdon, Devon	W, Sn	Feasibility studies complete, public inquiry under way
Africa	*Burundi*			
	Government	Musongati plateau	Ni, Cu	Feasibility studies under way for possible 2 million tonnes a year operation
	Egypt			
	Sinai Manganese	Sinai	Mn, Fe, Mn	Kaiser is undertaking a feasibility study
	Malagasy Republic			
	Kraomita Malagasy	Andriamena	Fe, Cr	Loan for pilot plant for 60,000 tonnes a year operation
	South Africa			
	Shell South Africa	Upington, CP	W	Feasibility studies
	Sudan			
	BRGM/GMRD	Red Sea Hills	W, Pb, Zr	Feasibility studies
	Uganda			
	Kilembe Mines	Kilembe	Cu, Co	Sherritt Gordon is undertaking feasibility study of cobalt project
	Upper Volta			
	Somitam	Tambao	Mn	Seeking finance for 500,000 tonnes a year operation
	Zaire			
	Soc. Miniere de Tenke-Fungurume	Shaba	Cu conc., Co	Re-evaluation of possible development with 2000 tonnes a year Co

	Somikivu	Kiru	Nb	
	Zimbabwe			
	Mimosa Mining	Shabani	Pt, Ni	Evaluating results of pilot testing
	Rio Tinto Mining	Zinco Hartley	Pt, Ni, Cu	Pilot plant testing
Asia	*India*			
	Ferro Alloys Corp.	Randia, Orissa	Fe, Cr	New development at existing plant 50,000 tonnes a year Fe, Cr
	Orissa Mining Corp.	Keonjhar, Orissa	Fe, Cr	Austrian/Finnish assistance for 1983 completion of new plant at Pamnipal
	Philippines			
	Ferrochrome Philippines	Tagdoen, Misamis Or	Fe, Cr	1983 completion of Herdis/Voest Alpine plant to handle Acoje concentrates
	Benguet/CMI	Masinloc, Zambales	Cr concentrates	$11 million plant expansion, completion date 1985, for additional reserves
	Thailand			
	Phadaeng	Mae Sot, Tak	Zr, Cd	Thai/Vielle Montagne joint venture to produce zinc and 500 tonnes a year Col. completion 1985
	Sirithair Scheelite/ Stora Kopparbera	Doi Mok	WO_3	New development planned to produce 430 tonnes a year WO_3
	Turkey			
	Etibank	Elazig, Guleman	Fe, Cr	Expansion of Fe, Cr smelter from 44,000 tonnes a year to 150,000 tonnes

BIBLIOGRAPHY

'A Brief Guide to Mineral Resources in Africa', *Africa* (79) (March 1979)

Alexander, John and Richard Hattersley (1982) *Australian Mining, Minerals and Oil*, David Ell Press, Sydney

American Chemical Society (1973) *Chemistry in the Economy*, American Chemical Society and National Science Foundation, Washington, DC

American Institute of Mining, Metallurgical and Petroleum Engineers, Inc. (1975) *Industrial Minerals and Rocks* (Nonmetallics other than fuels), American Institute of Mining, Metallurgical and Petroleum Engineers, New York, NY

American University, Foreign Area Studies (1979) *Zaire, a Country Study*, 3rd edn, Foreign Area Studies, American University, Washington, DC

Amsbaugh, Jeffrey K. (1982) 'Mining the Seas for Metals', *Materials Engineering* (March)

Anders, Gerhard, W. Philip Gramm, S. Charles Maurice and Charles W. Smithson (1980) *The Economics of Mineral Extraction*, Praeger, New York, NY

Andrews, R.H. (1962) *Cobalt*, HMSO, London

Archer, A.A. (1973) 'Progress and Prespects of Marine Mining', *Mining Engineering, 25* (12)

Aron, J. and Co. *Annual Review of Platinum and Palladium*, New York (various issues)

Aschmann, H. (1970) 'The Natural History of a Mine', *Economic Geography* (April)

Bach R.O. *et al.* (1967) 'Lithium and Lithium Compounds' in A. Standen (ed.), *Encyclopedia of Chemical Technology*, vol. 12, 2nd edn, Interscience, New York, NY

Banks, F.E. (1977) 'National Resource Availability, Some Economic Aspects', *Resources Policy* (March)

Barbier, Claude (1971) *The Economics of Tungsten*, Metal Bulletin, London

Barksdale, J. (1966) *Titanium, Its Occurrence, Chemistry and Technology*, 2nd edn, Ronald Press, New York, NY

Barr, Robert Q. (1979) 'Review of Tungsten Production Prices, and Applications in 1978', *Journal of Metals, 31* (5)

——(1980) 'Molybdenum Statistics and Technology – 1979', *Journal of Metals, 32* (4)

——(1981) 'Molybdenum in 1980', *Journal of Metals, 33* (4)

Bartlett, E.S., H.W. Barr and J.L. McCall (1980) 'Germanium Supply and Demand', Report No. JO199132, Battelle-Columbus Laboratories

Bazdarich, Michael (1978) 'Inflation and Monetary Accommodation in the Pacific Basin', Federal Reserve Bank of San Francisco, *Review* (Summer)

Belli, Y., Raja K. Misra, K. Kubarych and M. Okada (1981) 'The Effect of Vanadium plus Titanium on the Magnetic and Mechanical Properties of Fe-Cr-Co Hard Magnets', *Materials Science and Engineering, 47*

Bergsten, C. Fred (1973) 'The Threat from the Third World', *Foreign Policy, II*

——(1974a) 'The New Era in World Commodity Markets', *Challenge, 17*

——*(1974b) 'Oil is Not* the Exception', *Foreign Policy, 14*, 86-90

——(1975) 'The U.S. Must Now Deal with Other Cartels', *New York Times*,

1 June
Beus, A.A. (1962) *Beryllium: Evaluation of Deposits during Prospecting and Exploratory Work* (trans. by F. Lachman), W.H. Freeman, San Francisco, Calif.
Blanco, J.L. (1978) 'Port Nickel Refinery in Production', *World Mining* (March)
Blanco, J.L. and B.M. Holliday (1981) 'Energy Swings at Nickel', *Journal of Metals, 33* (4)
Bradley, Elihu F. (compiler) (1979) *Source Book on Materials for Elevated Temperature Applications*, American Society for Metals, Metals Park, Ohio
Brett, John (1978) 'Electroplating: Choosing the Right Materials and Techniques', *Metals and Materials* (January)
Briggs, J.Z. and T.D. Parker (1965) 'The Super 12% Cr. Steels', in Climax Molybdenum Co., *The Super 12% Cr. Steels*
Brink, J.W. and L. Van Wambeke (1974) 'World Resources of Mercury', *Congress Internacional de Mercurio, 1*
Brooks, David B. (1965) *Supply and Competition in Minor Metals*, Resources for the Future Inc., Johns Hopkins Press
Bruning, R.J. (1980) 'Government Policies and Mining Exansion', *Mines Magazine* (October)
Buchanan, D.C. (1975) *Chromite Production from the Bushveld Complex and its Relationship to the Ferrochromium Industry*, University of Witwatersrand, Johannesburg
Burman, R.W. (1977) 'Molybdenum – a Super Superalloy', *Journal of Metals, 29*, 12 (December)
Burrows, James C. (1971) *Cobalt: An Industry Analysis*, Charles River Associates, Charlestown, MA
Calaway, Lee and W.C.J. van Ronsburg (1982) 'US Strategic Minerals: Policy Options' *Resources Policy, 8*, 2 (June)
Canada, Department of Energy, Mines and Resources (1980) 'Imported Mineral Raw Materials: Guidelines for Research Policy', *Mineral Policy Sector Internal Report* MRJ 80/8, Ottawa
(1980) 'Catalytic Converters: Current Trends', *The Society of Automotive Engineers – Australasia* (May-June)
Centre d'information du cobalt (1960) *Cobalt Monograph*, Brussels
Chadwick, John R. (1979) 'Zambian Cobalt Gains Importance as World Source', *World Mining* (September)
Chandler, Harry E. (1979) 'Overview of Japanese Automotive Materials', *Metal Progress 116* (4)
—— (1980a) 'Challenges in Aerospace Materials and Processes During the 80's', *Metal Progress, 117* (3)
—— (1980b) 'A Look Ahead at Auto Materials and Processes in the 80's, *Metal Progress, 117* (6)
—— (1980c) 'The Next 20 Years in Materials and Process Engineering', *Metal Progress, 118* (4)
Chandler, Harry E. and Donald F. Baxter Jnr (annual) 'Technology Forecast', *Metal Progress, 113* (1) (January 1978); *115* (1) (January 1979); *117* (1) (January 1980); *119* (1) (January 1981)
Charles River Associates Inc. (1969) *Economic Analysis of the Tungsten Industry*, Cambridge, Mass.

Clarfield, Kenneth W., S. Jackson, J. Keeffe, M.A. Noble and A.P. Ryan (1975) *Eight Mineral Cartels: The New Challenge to Industrialized Nations*, Metals Week, New York, NY

Clark, Peter (1978) 'The Copper Metals – Some Recent Developments', *Metals Australasia* (January)

'The Coming Squeeze on Defense Industries', *The Morgan Guaranty Survey* (May 1981)

Commins, K. (1980) 'Worldwide Crises Threaten U.S. Supply of Strategic Materials', *Journal of Commerce* 8 April

Copper Development Association (1965a) 'Beryllium Copper', *Brochure No. 54*, CDA, Potters Bar

—— (1965b) 'The Nickel Silvers', *Brochure No. 71*, CDA, Potters Bar

Cranstone, D. and H.L. Martin (1973) 'Are Ore Discovery Costs Increasing?' *Canadian Mining Journal* (April)

'Critical Materials – How Big is the Problem?', *Materials Engineering* (June 1981)

Crossley, Frank (1978) 'A New Weight and Cost Saving Titanium Alloy', *Metal Progress, 114* (3)

Crowson, J. (1977) 'The U.K.Strategic Stockpile', *Metal Bulletin* (March)

Cuddington, John T. (1981) 'Money Income, and Causality in the United Kingdom', *Journal of Money, Credit and Banking, 13* (3)

Dancoisne, P. (1978) 'Spotlight on Manganese', *Metals and Materials* (June)

Darwin, G.E. and J.H. Buddery (1960) *Beryllium*, Butterworths, London

Davison, R.M. and R.F. Steigerwald (1979) 'The New Ferritic Stainless Steels', *Metal Progress, 115* (6)

Decker, R.F. (1981) 'Superalloys – Does Life Renew at 50?', *Journal of Metals, 33* (5)

De Mille, John B. (1947) *Straregic Minerals*, 1st edn, McGraw-Hill, New York, NY

Dorfler, R.R. and J.M. Laferty (1981) 'Review of Molybdenum Recovery Processes', *Journal of Metals, 33* (5)

Down C.G. and John Stocks (1977) 'Methods of Tailings Disposal', *Mining Magazine* (May)

Dowsing, R.J. (1979a) 'Scrap Management in a Volatile World Market', *Metals and Materials* (April)

—— (1979b) 'Spotlight on Molybdenum', *Metals and Materials* (April)

—— (1979c) 'Future Metal Strategy Part 1: Planning a Policy to AD2000', *Metals and Materials* (June)

—— (1979d) 'Spotlight on Titanium, Parts 1, 2 and 3', *Metals and Materials* (July/August, October and December)

—— (1979e) 'Future Metal Strategy, Parts I and II', *Metals and Materials* (August and September)

—— (1979f) 'Future Metal Strategy Part 2: Resources Adequate; Politics and Energy Will Pose the Problems', *Metals and Materials* (September)

—— (1980) 'The Platinum Group Metals, Parts I and II', *Metals and Minerals* (May and July)

Duffy, J.I. (1979) *Printing Inks, Developments Since 1975*, Noyes Data Corp., Park Ridge, NJ

Duke, V.W.A. (1979) *Cobalt, A Mineral Commodity Review*, Internal Memorandum, No. 6, Minerals Bureau, Department of Mines, Johannesburg

(February)

Eckbo, Paul Leo (1975) 'OPEC and the Experience of Previous International Commodity Cartels', MIT Energy Laboratory Working Paper No. 75-008WP, Cambridge, Mass.

Eigo, D.P., J.W. Franklin and G.H. Cleaver (1955) 'Lithium', *Engineering and Mining Journal, 155*

Energy, Mines and Resources Canada (1980) *Vanadium: An Imported Mineral Commodity* (December)

'Ensuring Britain's Access to Vital Resources', *Metals and Materials* (September 1979)

Evans, R.K. (1978) 'Spotlight on Vanadium', *Metals and Materials* (April)

——(1978/9) 'New Aerospace Materials Debut at Farnborough '78', *Metals and Materials* (December/January)

Fairclough, A.J. (1978) 'Metals Production, Recycling and the Environment', *Metals and Materials* (August)

Fisher, Franklin (1970) 'Test of Equality between Sets of Coefficients in Linear Regressions', *Econometrics* (March)

Fletcher, F.B. and J.W. Morrow (1980) 'Chrome-Molybdenum Steels Counter Rail Wear Without Costly Heat Treatment', *Metals and Materials* (July)

Frondel, C. (1957) 'Zirconium – Mineralogy and Geochemistry', *Advances in Nuclear Engineering*, Vol. 2, Part 2, Proceedings, 2nd edn, Nuclear Engineering and Science Congress, Philadelphia, Pa.

Frost and Sullivan Ltd *World Political Risk Forecast*, New York (various issues)

Gabe, David Russell (1978) *Principles of Metal Surface Treatment and Protection,* 2nd edn, Pergamon Press, Oxford

Gibson-Jarvie, Robert (1975) *The London Metal Exchange – A Commodity Market*, Woodhead-Faulkner Ltd, London

Gilbert, P.T. (1978) 'Copper Alloys for Offshore Applications', *The Metallurgist and Materials Technologist*

Gillson, J.L. (ed.) (1960) *Industrial Minerals and Rocks*, 3rd edn, AIME, New York, NY

Gilman, John J. (1979) 'Ferrous Metallic Glasses', *Metal Progress, 116* (2)

Godden, M. (1977) 'Aerospace Materials – A Survey of Reseach Topics', Can Met, *Physical Metallurgy Research Laboratories Report*, MRP/PMRL, 79/77 Ottawa

Goetzel, Claus G., John B. Rittenhouse and John B. Singletary (1965) *Space Materials Handbook*, Addison-Wesley, Reading, Mass.

Gold Fields Group, Consulting Engineers Division (1981) 'The Marketing of Metals and Minerals', *Coal, Gold and Base Minerals of Southern Africa* (September)

Goldwater, Leonard J. (1974) *Mercury, A History of Quicksilver*, York Press, Baltimore, Md.

Goss, Barry A. (1980) 'The Forward Pricing Function of the London Metal Exchange', *Applied Economics, 1*

Goth, J.W. (1980) 'The Costs of Regulation to the Metals Industry', *Journal of Metals, 32* (11)

Granger, C.W.J. (1969) 'Investigating Causal Relations by Econometric Models and Cross-Spectral Methods', *Econometrica, 37* (July)

Gray, Allen G. (1981) 'Substitution/Conservation Technology for Critical Materials', *Metal Progress* (December)

Greenfield, P. (1971) *Engineering Applications of Beryllium*, Monograph ME/7, Mills and Boon, London

Grieg, Ian (1981) 'The Changing Platinum Market', Southern African Metals and Minerals in a World Context, May 1981 Conference, Johannesburg

Grose, Robert and John Stack (1982) 'Non-Economic Risk Evaluation in Multinational Banks', *Working Paper No. 1-82*, Graduate School of Business Administration, University of Michigan

Guy, Albert G. (1959) *Elements of Physical Metallurgy*, Addision-Wesley, Reading, Mass.

Haendel, Dan, Gerald T. West and Robert G. Meadow (1975) *Overseas Investment and Political Risk*, The Foreign Policy Research Institute, Philadelphia, Pa.

Hampel, Clifford A (ed.) (1961) *Rare Metals Handbook*, 2nd edn, Reinhold Publishing Corp., London

Haner, F.T. (1975) 'Business Environment Risk Index', *Best's Review*, Property Liability Insurance edn (July)

Harrigan, A. (1976) 'The Ultimate Target', *National Review* (14 May)

Harvey, A.C. (1980) 'On Comparing Regression Models in Levels and First Differences', *International Economic Review, 21* (3)

Heisterkamp, F. (1978) 'Niobium Moves into High-speed Tool Steels', *Metals and Materials* (October)

Highberger, W.T. (1979) 'Advances in Manufacturing Technology for Titanium Aircraft Structures', *Metal Progress, 115* (3)

Hillier, G. and N.D. Knight (1978) 'The Australian Tungsten Mining Industry', *Australian Mineral Industry Quarterly, 31*

Hodger, F Galen (1978) 'Improved Stability Nickel-Base Alloys Meet New CPI Requirements', *Metal Progress, 113* (2)

Hoefer, J.N. and D.W. Bange (978) 'A Graph Theoretic Model of Cartel Formation and Structure', *Professional Geographer, 30,* 190-8

Honkala, R.A. and K.R. Knoblock (1980) 'A Cartographic Look at Constraints to Mineral Exploration and Development', *Mining Congress Journal* (February)

Hotelling, Harold (1931) 'The Economics of Exhaustible Resources', *Journal of Political Economy* (April)

Hudson Institute (1981) 'Index of Political Tension 1970-1980', *Commodity Journal* (June)

Interagency Task Force (1979) *Report on the Issues Identified in the Nonfuel Minerals Policy Review*, Draft Report, US Government Printing Office, Washington, DC

International Conference on Titanium, First (London, 1968) (1970) *The Science, Technology and Application of Titanium*, Proceedings, 1st edn, Oxford, NH

International Iron and Steel Institute (1981) *Chromium and the Steel Industry*, IISI, Brussels, Belgium

International Strategic Metals Ltd (1981) *Prospectus*, New York, NY

Irving, Robert R. (1980) 'What Demands Lie Ahead for Our Metallurgists?', *Iron Age* (21 July)

Jacobs, Rodney L., Edward E. Leamer and Michael P. Ward (1979) 'Difficulties with Testing for Causation', *Economic Inquiry, XVII* (July)

Jacobson, D.M. and D.S. Evans (1983) 'The Supply Economics of Germanium', *The Metallurgist and Materials Technologist* (March)

Johnson, F.N. (ed.) (1975) *Lithium Research and Therapy*, Academic Press, London

Kabrin, Stephen J. (1981) 'Political Assessment by International Firms: Models or Methodologies?', *Journal of Policy Modeling, 3* (2)

Kearney, J.P. (1981) 'Recent Developments in the South African Ferro-chrome Industry', *Erzmetall, 34* (4)

Kerr, Paul Francis (1946) *Tungsten Mineralization in the United States*, Waverly Press, Baltimore, Md.

Kirkham, Ross (1979) 'Engine Parts into the Eighties, Part I – Bearings', *The Society of Automotive Engineers – Australasia* (November-December)

Klass, Michael W. (1980) *Internatinal Mineral Cartels and Embargoes: Policy Implications for the United States*, Praeger, New York, NY

Kundig, Konrad, J.A. (1981) 'The Tungsten Market – From Chaos to Stability', *Journal of Metals, 33* (5)

Kunert, D.I. (1981) 'Africa: Soviet Strategy and Western Counter-strategy', *Southern Africa Forum*, Occasional Paper, *1*

Lamey, Carl A. (1966) *Metallic and Industrial Mineral Deposits*, McGraw-Hill, New York, NY

Landel, Robert F. and Alan Renbaum (eds.) (1956) *Chemistry in Space Research*, American Elsevier, New York, NY

Landolt, P.E. (1951) 'Lithium Minerals Provide Unique Industrial Raw Materials', *Mining Engineering, 3*

Landsberg, Hans H., Leonard L. Fischman and Joseph L. Fisher (1963) *Resources in America's Future: Patterns for Resources for the Future, of Requirements and Availabilities, 1960-2000,* Johns Hopkins Press for Resources for the Future, Baltimore, Md.

Larsen, Judith (1981) 'Comparative Philosophy of Environmental Regulations', *Journal of Metals, 33* (3)

Le May, I. (1980) *Advances in Materials Technology in the Americas – 1980*, Vols. 1 and 2, American Society of Mechanical Engineers, New York, NY

Long, Ngo V. (1975) 'Resource Extraction Under the Uncertainty about Possible Nationalization', *Journal of Economic Theory, 10* (1)

Lula, R.A. (1979) 'Effects of Materials Shortages on Stainless Steel Technology', *Metal Progress, 116* (5)

Lustman, B. and F. Kerze, Jr. (1955) *The Metallurgy of Zirconium*, McGraw-Hill, New York, NY

McLendon, Godon (1980) *Get Really Rich in the Coming Super Metals Boom*, Simon and Schuster, New York, NY

Meermans, Marcia J. (1982) 'U.S. Materials Policy – Do We Have a Fighting Chance in the Resource War', *Materials Engineering* (January)

Messler, R.W. Jr. and C.A. Paez (1980) 'Low Cost Advanced Titanium Airframe Structures viaWelding', *Metal Progress, 117* (3)

Metallurrgical Society of AIME (1981a) *Titanium '80*, Metallurgical Society of AIME, Warrendale, Penn.

—— (1981b) *Titanium and Titanium Alloys, Scientific and Technological Aspects*, Plenum Publishing Co., New York, NY

Meyer, H.E. (1981) 'How We're Fixed for Strategic Materials', *Fortune, 103* (3)

Michalski, Wolfgang (1978) 'Future Mineral Supplies – Politics, Not Lack of Ore, May Create Scarcity', *World Mining* (September)

Miller, James A. (1980) *Struggle for Survival: Strategic Materials and the West*, American African Affairs Association, Washington, DC

Mineral Bureau (1980) *South Africa's Significance in World Mineral Supply*, Johannesburg (January)

Minkler, Ward W. (1978) 'Titanium for Chemical Processing Equipment', *Metal Progress, 113* (2)

—— (1981) 'Titanium in 1980', *Journal of Metals, 33* (4)

Miska, Kurt, H. (1981) 'Tungsten in 1980', *Journal of Metals, 33* (4)

Mock, John A. (1980) 'Holding Down the Cost of Precious-metal Electroplates', *Materials Engineering* (April)

Mockler, W. (1978) 'High Temperature Metals for the Heat Treatment Industry', *Metals Australasia* (March)

Mohide, Thomas Patrick (1979) *Platinum Group Metals – Ontario and the World*, Ontario Mineral Policy Background Paper No. 7, Ottawa

Morgan, John D.J. (1980) 'The Non-fuel Mineral Position of the USA', *Resources Policy, 6* (1)

Muff, Folf (1978) *The Antimony Deposits in the Murchison Range of the North-eastern Transvaal, Republic of South Africa*, Gebruder Borntraeger, Berlin

Nappi, Carmine (1979) *Commodity Market Controls*, D.C. Heath, Lexington, Mass.

National Academy of Science (1980) *Supply and Use Patterns for the Platinum-Group Metals*, National Materials Advisory Board Publication NMAB-359, National Academy of Science, Washington, DC

National Association of Secondary Material Industries (1967) *The Nonferrous Scrap Metal Industry*, NASMI, New York, NY

Netschert, Bruce C. (1978) 'The Future Availability of Raw Materials', *Journal of Metals, 30* (8)

NSW Department of Mines (1965) *The Mineral Industry of New South Wales, No. 11, Cobalt* (April)

Osborne, D.K. (1976) 'Cartel Problems', *American Economic Review, 66* (5)

Ostensson, Olle (1980) 'What Future Holds for Swedish Mineral Production, Usage', *World Mining* (May)

Parkinson, P. (1980) 'By-Products Could Be a Trap', *Metal Bulletin* (16 September)

Parrish, M.A. (1980) 'Fuel Cells – A Survey', *Materials in Engineering, 2* (December)

Pazour, Donald (1980) 'Mexico Joins Moly League: Cumobabi Now Mining Ore', *World Mining* (July)

Petersen, U. and R.S. Maxwell (1979) 'Historical Mineral Production and Price Trends', *Mining Engineering* (January)

Pierce, David A. and Larry D. Haugh (1979) 'Causality in Temporal Systems', *Journal of Econometrics, 5*

Pindyck, Robert S. (1977) 'Cartel Pricing and the Structure of the World Bauxite Market', *Bell Journal of Economics, 8* (2)

—— (1978) 'Gains to Producers from the Cartelization of Exhaustible Resources', *Review of Economics and Statistics, 60* (2)

Pings, W.B. (1972) 'Titanium, Parts 1 and 2', *Colorado School of Mines Industries Bulletin, 15* (4) and (5)

Pipgras, John J. and H.J. Metz (1980) 'Managing Critical Materials in the 80's',

Metal Progress, 117 (6)
Promisel, N.E. and Allen G. Gray (1982) 'USA Tackles Critical Materials', Resources Policy, 8 (2)
Radetzki, Marian (1977) 'Mineral Commodity Stabilization, the Producers' View', *Resources Policy* (June)
'Recovery and Recycling', *Processing* (March 1981)
Reddy, Bernard J. (1980) 'Cobalt into the 1980s', *Journal of Metals, 32* (4)
—— (1981) 'Cobalt Imbalance in 1980', *Journal of Metals, 33* (4)
Reeve, D.J. (1980) 'Applications of Hard Chromium Plating', *Metals Australasia* (September)
Reinsch, W.A. and H.W. Rosenberg (1980) 'Three Recent Developments in Titanium Alloys', *Metal Progress* (March)
Ridinger, David C. (1980) 'Cost of Regulation to the Mining Industry', *Mining Congress Journal* (February)
Robinson, George, H. (1981) 'Future of Alloy Steels in the Automobile', *Metal Progress, 119* (5)
Rust, T.M., B.B. Seth and R.E. Warner (1979) 'Operating Experience with Titanium Steam Turbine Blades', *Metal Progress, 116* (2)
Rummel, R.J. and D.A. Heenan (1978) 'How Multinationals Analyze Political Risk', *Harvard Business Review, 56*
Ryan, B.C. (1980) 'Mining Finance Houses – Changes in the 80's', *JASSA* (2) (August)
Salant, Stephen W. and Dale W. Henderson (1978) 'Market Anticipations of Government Policies and the Price of Gold', *Journal of Political Economy, 81* (4)
Sanders, T.H. (1978) 'Aluminium-Lithium Alloys: Low Density and High Stiffness', *Metal Progress, 113* (3)
Schillmoller, C.M. and H.P. Klein (1981) 'Selecting and Using Some High Technology Stainless Steels', *Metal Progress, 119* (2)
Schlabach, Thomas D. (1980) 'Critical Materials and Substitution Strateges in the Communications Industry', *Metal Progress* (February)
Schmalensee, Richard (1976) 'Resource Exploitation Theory and the Behavior of the Oil Cartel', *European Economic Review* 7 (3)
Schmitz, K.H. (1979) 'Nickel Injection for Lower-cost Stainless Steel', *Metals and Materials* (April)
Schwer, R.E. (1981) 'Deficiencies of the US Materials Stockpile', *Journal of Metals, 33* (12)
See, J. Bruce (1980) 'Developments in Chromium – 1979', *Journal of Metals, 32* (4)
Shaw, Stuart W.K. (1979) 'INO939: A Corrosion-Resistant Alloy for Industrial and Marine Turbine Blades', *Metal Progress, 115* (3)
Sheffield Metallurgical and Engineering Association (1980) 'Ensuring Supplies of Strategic Alloying Elements for Special Steelmaking (Part 2)', *Metals and Materials* (September)
Shepherd, A.C.C. (1981) 'Chrome Ore and Ferro-Chrome in Southern Africa and World Markets', Southern African Metals and Minerals in a World Context Conference, Johannesburg (May)
Shimkin, D.B. (1953) *Minerals – A Key to Soviet Power*, Harvard University Press, Cambridge, Mass.

Shirley, Joseph F. (1978) 'It is Time to Look at Moly Again: Optimizing the By-Product Circuit', *World Mining* (July)
—— (1979) 'Optimizing the By-product Circuit', *World Mining* (July)
Simons, Eric N. (1969) *A Dictionary of Alloys*, Frederic Muller, New York, NY
Sims, Christopher (1972) 'Money Income and Causality', *American Economic Review* (September)
Sinclair Securities Company (1980) *Strategic Materials – A Guide*, New York
Smirnov, V.I. (1977) *Ore Deposits of the USSR*, Vol. 11, Pitman, London
Smith, Ben (1980) 'Long-Term Contract Arrangements and Financing Arrangements for Mineral Developments', Australia-Japan Economic Relations Research Project, Research Paper No. 72, Australian National University, Canberra (September)
Smith, D.F. and E.F. Clatworthy (1981) 'The Development of High Strength Low Expansion Alloys', *Metal Progress, 119* (4)
Society Emery Policy Advisory Committee (1981) 'The Cost of Present and Future Emission Controls on Australian Cars', *The Society of Automotive Engineers – Australasia* (March/April)
Stewart, R.E. (1981) 'The Competitive Position of Chilean Copper Mines in the 1980's', *The Northern Miner* (12 February)
Strauss, Simon (1978) 'Stockpiling: An Historical Summary', *Journal of International Law and Economics, 12* (2)
Stuckley, John A. (1980) 'The Role of Marketing Arrangements in the Evaluation and Finnancing of Mining Projects', Australia-Japan Economic Relations Research Project, Australian National University, Research Paper No. 71 (September)
Szuprowicz, Bohdan (1981) 'Critical Materials Cut-offs Feared', *High Technology* (November/December)
Tien, J.K., T.E. Howson, G.L. Chen and X.S. Xie (1980) 'Cobalt Availability and Superalloys', *Journal of Metals, 32* (10)
Tilton, John E. (1977) 'Cartels and Embargoes', Chapter 6 in John E. Tilton, *The Future of Non-Fuel Minerals*, Brookings Institution, Washington, DC
Tupper, Nathan G., Jerome K. Elbaum and H.M. Burte (1978) 'Opportunities for Cost-Affordable Titanium Aerospace Structures', *Journal of Metals, 30* (9)
US Bureau of Mines (1981) *Commodity Data Summary*, Washington, DC
Van Rensburg, W.C.J. (1974) 'South Africa's Future Role as a Supplier of Raw Materials to the World', *Southern African Journal of African Affairs*
Van Rensburg, W.C.J. and D.A. Pretorious (1977) *South Africa's Strategic Minerals – Pieces on a Continental Chess Board*, Valiant Publishers, Johannesburg
Varon, B. and K. Takeuchi (1974) 'Developing Countries and Non-Fuel Minerals', *Foreign Affairs* (April)
Verink, Ellis D. Jr. (1980) 'Non-Fuel Materials – The Next National Crisis', *Journal of Metals, 32* (4)
Wang, K.P. (1975) *The People's Republic of China, A New Industrial Power with a Strong Mineral Base*, US Bureau of Mines, Washington, DC
Watson, S.A. (1978) 'Nickel – Its Future in the Metal Finishing Industry', *Metals Australasia* (February)
Webb, M. (1979) *The Chemistry, Biochemistry and Biology of Cadmium*, Elsevier/North-Holland Biomedical Press

Webster, R. Terrence (1978) 'Zirconium for Chemical Processing Applications', *Metal Progress, 113* (2)
Wikle, Keith G. (1978) 'Combating Wear with Beryllium Copper', *Metal Progress, 113* (6)
Wye, Alan (1982) 'Minor Metal Trading: A Personal View', *Metal Bulletin Monthly* (July)
Zellner, A. (1979) 'Causality and Econometrics', in K. Brunner and A.H. Meltzer (eds.), *Three Aspects of Policy and Policymaking: Knowledge, Data and Institutions*, North Holland, Amsterdam

INDEX

Note: The index includes name of companies but not mines. For the latter, look under the appropriate country, e.g. Bolivia: lithium production *and* Bolivia: mines.

For Product Safety Concerns and Information please contact our EU representative GPSR@taylorandfrancis.com Taylor & Francis Verlag GmbH, Kaufingerstraße 24, 80331 München, Germany